Jo Parker - *A brief biography*

In a way, Jo Parker's whole life has been in water. From earliest childhood, she delighted in directing little streams of water and building dams. While studying for her degree in civil engineering, Jo took a vacation job with one of Britain's river authorities. This convinced her that she should specialise in water engineering and, after she had gained her BSc, she joined Thames Water in their design office.

The job of managing front line operations, involving the overseeing of manual labour, seemed to elude her, so she jumped at the chance to spend a year in the heart of Afghanistan working to rebuild the irrigation systems of a remote and beautiful valley there. Her incredible adventures during this extraordinary year are chronicled in vivid detail in her book, Water under the Bridge.

After the Afghan adventure, Jo found herself pitched into the middle of the Bosnian War where, for some three months, she worked virtually on the front line, reconstructing vital water supplies to the besieged city of Sarajevo. For this she was awarded the MBE.

Jo is now Head of Asset Management for Three Valleys Water, with responsibility for the installation and maintenance of billions of pounds worth of water pipes and equipment. As a broadcaster she has recently appeared in the series, "Secrets of the Ancients" on BBC2, where she was required to reproduce the way in which the hanging Gardens of Babylon might have been irrigated. Also on BBC2, she took part in the competitive series, "The Great Egg Race" and also an Open Door programme on Women Engineers.

Jo has been interviewed for the BBC about her work by both Jenny Murray on "Woman's Hour" and Matthew Parris on "S.O.S." and has been referred to in the media as "The Kate Adie of the water industry"!

She travels extensively, addressing international groups on vital water related subjects and is also an excellent musician. Her chosen instrument is the double bass, as with this she is able to enjoy playing both jazz and classical music. She lives in a beautiful country cottage, which is, naturally, situated on the banks of a gently flowing river. Her companion is a ginger cat named Zebedee, whom she rescued from a Pakistani slum on her way to Afghanistan and who shared in all her amazing adventures there.

Watershed Publishing UK

Kingfisher Cottage, Drayton Ford
Rickmansworth, Herts WD3 8FE

Published in Great Britain 2003
By Watershed Publishing

For further information about Water under the Bridge
Please visit us at **www.watershedpublishing.com**

ISBN 0-9545366-0-6

Water under the Bridge

Jo Parker

Acknowledgments

To Paula who believed in me. Jenni who got me started on this book, Valentine who finished it off. Jill, who kept everything in order whilst I was away and to my two sisters who are the best role models anyone could have

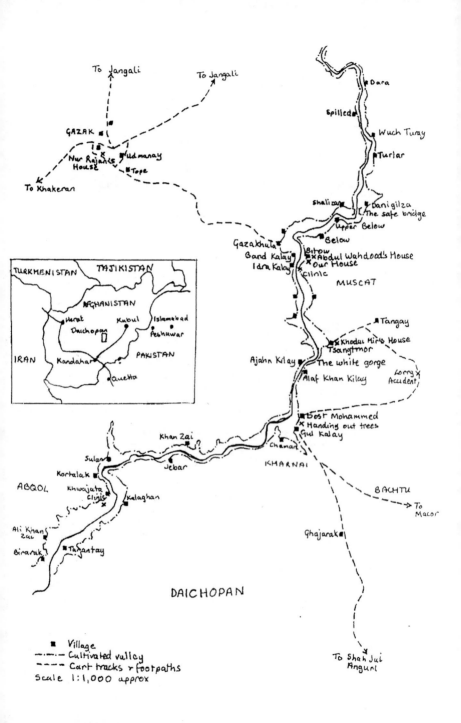

Chapter One

I've always been terrified of heights but here I was, crowded into an ancient Mercedes truck with a bunch of holy warriors and two other Englishwomen, as the unstable vehicle creaked and groaned its way along a narrow mountain road. Most roads in Afghanistan would be classed as rough farm tracks back in England. As the truck crawled along the side of the mountain at walking pace, I stole an occasional glance over the edge of the road into the valley below. Most of the land there was parched dry, but every so often there was a bright green patch, where some enterprising farmers had been able to irrigate their fields. This was our fourth day of travelling through some of Afghanistan's most dangerous territory, dangerous because we had entered the country illegally, and because we were working with the Mujahideen. The year was 1989 and, although the Russian invaders had withdrawn, the communist government in Kabul was still to be overthrown and the Mujahideen were intent on doing it. I didn't know it at the time, but many of the heavily armed men in the Mercedes truck were destined to be Taliban fighters.

Afghanistan has always been a land of many tribes, constantly engaging in bitter feuds. A number of the main towns on our most direct route through the country were in the hands of factions that would not take kindly to our Pashtu escort. As a result, we were forced to take this circuitous route from Pakistan to our destination, the valley of Daichopan. I kept telling myself that our Afghan driver knew what he was doing, but I was not convinced. Suddenly, to my horror, the road beneath us began to subside and, like some huge, mortally wounded beast, the truck wobbled before sliding over the edge of the road and tumbling down the steep mountain slope, carrying everything and everyone with it. As I was flung about in the crashing truck I began to lose consciousness; my last coherent thought was: 'Why on earth did I ever come on this crazy trip to Afghanistan? '

The answer was my sheer stubbornness and determination, qualities I inherited from my father. I was born in Germany, where he was a colonel in the British army. His task there was to help establish new radio systems, having previously worked in some mysterious undercover operation in the Middle East. At my birth, the doctors did not expect me to live, as I was a rhesus baby, turning blue as my blood clotted from the fatal mix inherited from my parents. The only hope was a total transfusion but, after two attempts, my blood still refused to clear. I clung tenaciously to life and it was decided to try one last transfusion. Miraculously, it worked. I grew into a normal healthy child and, when I was still quite small, we moved back to England, into a large, rambling house near Epping Forest.

I enjoyed school and joined in as many after-school activities as I could. As both jazz and classical music appealed to me, I took up playing the bass. It seemed to me to be an instrument equally at home in either a jam session or a concert hall. Once I had passed my driving test I was allowed the rare privilege of parking a car in the school grounds, having convinced the headmistress that my instrument was too heavy to carry from the main road.

My mother was a maths teacher and this, coupled with my father's technical background, made it almost inevitable that, although I enjoyed most subjects, my particular favourites were science and maths. When the time came for me to leave school, I decided I wanted to study something related to science or technology. It occurred to me that, for my university degree course, civil engineering might be an interesting combination of science and creativity. I soon discovered that most people considered this a totally unsuitable choice for a girl, but my parents saw nothing wrong in it and, anyway, I've always enjoyed swimming against the current of popular opinion.

All my life, even as a tiny child, I've been fascinated by water. Not just splashing around in it like most kids, but building miniature dams and irrigation schemes. So when, at university, I had the chance of a vacation job working as a river engineer, I grabbed it with both hands, and my consuming passion developed into a career. I confess to being fascinated by water, by its clarity, its purity, its power to save life and yet to destroy cities, wash away a landscape or poison a community. Civil engineers are the high priests of water, holding the secrets that can tame this potentially lethal force behind huge dams or direct it, with all docility, to every householder's tap.

My career began at Thames Water, where I was involved in the designing of sewage works. This may not be everyone's idea of the perfect job, but I loved it and it gave me the opportunity to live and work in the beautiful city of Oxford. I managed to find a wonderful little house on an island in the middle of the river Thames and, for a time, my life was idyllic. My job at Thames Water gave me the chance to get to know the men who spent their every working day at the plants and I came to appreciate the pride they had in their job and the depth of their knowledge. Unfortunately, those in management at the time failed to share my view. Time and again I applied to run one of the water works or sewage plants that I had designed, but I always seemed to hit an invisible wall. I was told, unofficially, that it was considered too much of a risk to put a woman in charge of male manual workers.

One day, something happened that was to change my life. In one of the water industry's trade magazines I caught sight of an advertisement for an organisation called Registered Engineers for Disaster Relief (REDR), which sent highly qualified engineers to disaster areas all over the world. I realised that this could give me the opportunity I was looking for, a way to prove to the men in suits that I could manage manual labour, albeit abroad. Enthusiastically I signed up but, although I attended a few meetings, nothing much seemed to be happening and, after a time, I almost forgot about REDR.

Two years went by, as I moved through different departments and up the corporate ladder. Each time I was promoted, it was hinted that I had been tipped for the top. Unfortunately, it wasn't exactly the top I wanted. General Business Development, Commercial Development and Marketing might be just the roles some people longed for, but my idea of making it was being a manager in operations. Actually running a water works was what I considered to be really rewarding work. So it wasn't so much a glass ceiling that I bumped up against, more of a glass wall. I could get promotion, but not in the direction that I wanted to go. Then, one bright June morning, I returned to my office after a four-day break to find a pile of messages on my desk. One of them simply said 'Phone Paola Sandersley'. For a moment I couldn't think who this was, then I remembered that she was the director of the Register of Engineers for Disaster Relief. I thought she probably wanted to invite me to one of REDR's training sessions but, when I called her, it was something much more dramatic.

'Jo, I've got an assignment for you.'

'Where?'

'Afghanistan.'

'How long for?'

'Nine months.'

'When do they want me to leave?'

'As soon as possible.'

'What will I be paid?'

'£300 a month.'

'OK, I'll do it.'

'Hang on a moment, are you sure?'

I was very sure. The job involved designing and implementing irrigation and sanitation systems, as well as building a vital footbridge across a wide river. Not only would this trip give me the chance to do something really useful, but I could also prove something to the suits at Thames Water. By taking this job in Afghanistan, not only would I be in charge of male manual workers, but they would be men from a society where women are traditionally kept within the household and forbidden to speak to any man outside their own family. If I could handle Afghan male workers for nine months to a year, it would prove beyond all doubt that I could manage manual labour.

Working among the Afghans would place me in a unique and privileged position. Although I would be treated as an 'honorary' man, I would also be able to see how the local Afghan women lived. No Western male would ever be permitted to speak with them, yet this was essential for the engineer to do, for the problem of household sanitation is more important to the women than to the men. After all, the men can use the whole valley as a toilet if they want to.

Although I had been contacted through REDR, it was a charity called Health Unlimited that had need of my services. I met them at their central London offices, which were located in an imposing building just south of the Thames. However, as I made my way up several staircases and down various corridors, the surroundings became less and less imposing. Finally I found myself in Health Unlimited's office. It consisted of a very small room with a couple of chairs and an ancient filing cabinet. Although the staff there were very charming, it was obvious that they knew nothing about engineering. However, they seemed perfectly happy to take me on REDR's recommendation, assuming that my basic technical competence would overcome my lack of experience of working in primitive locations.

I had never been involved in aid work before and so, before I met them, I half-imagined that my co-workers would be Amazonian women, able to knock out the odd Mujahideen with their bare fists. They turned out to be quite normal, just like me. Sarah, a qualified midwife and our team's leader, was tall and well built. Brought up in the country, she loved riding and walking, a decided advantage in Afghanistan, a country with almost no motorised transport. Caroline, the doctor, was very different. She lived in London and loved parties and dancing. Small and slim, she was practical and efficient, yet with just the right degree of sympathy needed by a doctor. As I had to deal with several major problems before setting off for Afghanistan, Sarah and Caroline went on ahead to Quetta, a town in south-west Pakistan close to the Afghan border which was to be our jumping-off point for Afghanistan.

My first problem was that Health Unlimited seemed permanently short of funds. This was to cause not only myself, but also Sarah and Caroline, considerable difficulties for the next year. I was the first engineer the charity had dealt with, so they had no engineering equipment for me to take out. As they seemed concerned about whether they could afford to pay me my £300 a month, there appeared little chance of them finding the cash to purchase any equipment for me. However, now that I had committed myself to the trip, I was determined that nothing should prevent me from going, so I had to beg and borrow what equipment I could, only paying for it when all else failed. To add to my concerns, I discovered that Health Unlimited had made no provision to have my supplies sent out ahead of me. It was bad enough having to struggle to the airport with my personal luggage, consisting of enough clothing for a year in one of the world's wildest countries, where the climate ranged from searing heat to ten degrees of frost and snow several feet deep. Now I found that I'd also got to carry everything I needed for the job – books, equipment, the lot.

The night before I was due to fly out from London, I stayed with my friend Jenni in Bloomsbury, so that, the next morning, I would be able to take the underground all the way to Heathrow airport. We stayed up until the early hours of the morning working out what I could jettison to cut down on my luggage, as I could see that I was going to be well into an excess baggage charge. Lots of my personal things had to go, but I was still left with one enormous suitcase full of equipment and clothes plus my 'hand luggage', a single bag containing all the books I thought I might need to refer to which made it almost too heavy to lift. I also had to carry the four-foot tripod for my surveying level.

Early in the morning we struggled down into the tube with my luggage. After nearly an hour's journey, we struggled up again, into the airport. The woman at the check-in desk was not of a generous nature.

She was a real 'battle-axe' and positively glowed with satisfaction on discovering that my luggage for the hold was well overweight. She then demanded that I put my cabin baggage on the scale. This was the one with the books in. My heart sank. The scales sank too, by twenty kilos. Almost gleefully, Battle-Axe demanded £240 for the excess baggage. Although I had a credit card with me, I wasn't sure if there was sufficient in my current account to repay it in my absence. I used every trick in the book on Battle-Axe. Acting the innocent, I pretended not to know about the baggage allowance. I argued that Health Unlimited must have made arrangements with the airline, although I knew full well they hadn't. Finally I tried to gain her sympathy by explaining that I was working for a charity. She was without charity. All she was prepared to do was delay my check-in for an hour, to give me a chance to phone Health Unlimited and get them to agree to pay the excess baggage charge. Of course, I should have known there would be no one in the office as early as half past eight in the morning and, sure enough, there was no reply to my phone call.

My friend Jenni was amazed. 'What kind of organisation are you working for? They make no arrangements to get your equipment flown out and they don't even have anyone on call in case of emergency?' I think she really began to wonder if I knew what I was doing. I kept ringing the charity and, just before nine o'clock, I got through to someone who asked me if there was anything I could jettison. I told him I'd already thrown out a load of stuff that I should really have been taking with me. Anyway, there was no time for me to repack and the only item which was separately wrapped was the tripod. Reluctantly I agreed to leave it behind, although how I was going to build a bridge without it I did not know.

As the plane gathered speed down the runway, I wondered what on earth I was doing. I was still relatively young, unattached and with a wonderful life in Oxford. I had a beautiful house and my beloved music. The thesis for my MBA had been completed just two days before and, with my new qualification, I could opt for all sorts of highly paid jobs.

Instead I was off to some remote village in the Afghan mountains with no electricity, no running water, no transport and no sanitation unless I built it myself. Added to this, we would be snowed in for the entire winter, without any contact with the outside world.

I stepped off the plane from London into an extraordinary world. I had visited northern Pakistan some years before with my mother, but I'd never experienced anything like this. Quetta's population had been swollen by huge numbers of refugees and charitable organisations and its narrow streets were jammed with traffic at every hour of the day. There were donkey carts, brightly coloured three-wheelers, highly decorated lorries that looked as though they belonged in a fairground, and camels. The noise was tremendous, and the traffic appeared to move at random, yet at such a slow pace that there seemed little danger of accidents. At the side of every road fruit sellers sat cross-legged on carts full of peaches, apples, grapes and melons, while other men squatted, chatting to each other or grilling sweetcorn in pans of charcoal. It wasn't just the local people who looked extraordinary. After a long, exhausting flight, I arrived in Quetta a bedraggled wreck in fleece-lined boots and a shalwa kameez, the long shirt and baggy trousers traditional in that area.

As soon as I met up with Sarah and Caroline again, they decided that first we should meet the Afghans we would be working with. We set off on a motorised rickshaw to visit the hotel where they were staying. I cannot imagine how anyone could describe the rundown building as a hotel. It lay down a maze of dark and dirty backstreets. In front of it was a barbecue belching clouds of thick blue-grey smoke, while young boys washed the dishes in bowls beside turgid gutters. My stomach heaved, as I was starting to suffer the first of many gastric upsets that would plague me throughout my first months in Afghanistan. However, I would not have missed this meeting for the world.

Although fighting continued in some parts of Afghanistan, I had been assured that the area where Health Unlimited worked was returning to normal. It was a river valley with an entirely agricultural economy but, during the war against the Russians, most of the men had been away fighting and a number of essential maintenance jobs had been left undone. There were several vital projects that had to be undertaken as swiftly as possible: getting the irrigation systems working properly again, improving sanitation, devising better flood control and, most importantly, building a new footbridge across the river. Although I was a chartered civil engineer with fifteen years' experience at Thames Water, I had never worked overseas, and I had to trust that I would have the necessary skills and equipment to handle these projects.

Health Unlimited had been running an aid programme in a valley in southern Afghanistan for five years. The previous teams had comprised medical and teaching staff, who had established a clinic and a school. Now, for the first time, the Afghans had asked for an engineer. The request had come from the local Mujahideen leader or warlord, Abdul Wahdood. This 'hotel' was where we were to meet him, together with others from the village where we would be working. Apparently Abdul was anxious to meet 'the engineer woman', and I certainly needed to meet him. The briefing I had received from Health Unlimited in London had been very sketchy, and I wanted a lot more information so that I could plan my work.

As I entered the 'hotel' my main concern was that my stomach wouldn't let me down. Throwing up in the middle of a meal might not create a very good first impression. We were led up a flight of steep, narrow stairs to the top floor where a series of rooms surrounded a central courtyard. It was very gloomy and I could sense the dirt everywhere around me. Compared to this, a dosshouse back in the UK would look like the Hilton. I guessed that the other two in the team were more used to such surroundings than I was: Sarah had been out to the valley twice before and Caroline had been an aid worker in Brazil. Health Unlimited had told me that they were going to arrange for a teacher and a dentist to join us at a later date.

The Afghans liked to give aid workers nicknames. Sarah had earned hers on one of her previous trips to Afghanistan. The jeep she was travelling in encountered a Russian tank and, at that time, any Afghan was regarded as an enemy of Russia. Her companions naturally jumped out of the jeep and ran for cover but Sarah had taken her shoes off on the journey and was still scrabbling about in the jeep for them when the tank opened fire. For this act of apparent bravery, Abdul Wahdood dubbed her 'Palowan' ('lion-hearted one'). Caroline and I would have our work cut out trying to beat that.

People have always shortened my name from Josephine to Jo. It seems to suit me and I like it. So I was fascinated to discover that 'Jo' is a word in Pashtu, the language of the valley we were headed for. It means 'barley', which seemed quite appropriate, as anything I did about flood control and irrigation would benefit the farmland where the local people grew their barley.

On meeting the seven Afghans who were to accompany us to Daichopan for the first time, I was somewhat confused. They all looked very much alike and all seemed to be called Abdul. All seven were very tall with big noses, curly black hair and big bushy beards. They wore dark-coloured shalwa kameezes and turbans, waistcoats, and what looked like an assortment of tea towels and tablecloths draped around them. To my surprise Abdul Wahdood, the warlord who was our host in the valley, was at only 24 the youngest of the group. I wondered how he managed to maintain his position of power.

All the Afghans were staying in one small room about ten feet square. How they were able to maintain any order there I never knew. There were cushions all around the edge of the room and a pile of brightly coloured mattresses in one corner. The only luggage was a small tin trunk, on top of which sat Abdul Wahdood's cassette recorder and a pile of tapes of Afghan music. I later discovered that the trunk contained a ten-piece tea service, so I figured that nobody had brought a change of clothes. Happily we didn't stay long in the overcrowded room but went downstairs to a restaurant in the basement. It was spartan but reasonably clean. There were formica-topped tables and plastic chairs. The alcoves were papered with newspapers and an electric fan kept the temperature down to an almost bearable level. I decided not to eat anything because of the state of my stomach, although the food looked delicious. There were piles of nan bread, plates of rice topped with raisins and caramelised onions, lamb on ferocious-looking kebab skewers and dishes of yoghurt. I sipped delicately at a Seven-Up while the others dug in. Afterwards we all went back upstairs for tea. I was a bit apprehensive, as these men used a tea-making process I had never seen before. They brought the water to the boil, added the tea leaves then brought the water to the boil again. I was afraid that this would make the tea very strong but in fact it turned out to be quite weak, which suited me fine. The tea was served with sweets that looked like almonds with a sugar coating and I was very tempted to try them. However, Sarah said they didn't taste half as good as the sugared almonds we get in England so, in view of my weak stomach, I resisted them.

My first impression of the Afghans was that I was really going to enjoy working with them. They seemed warm and friendly and loved practical jokes and visual humour. One of them did a hysterically funny impression of a health worker taking a pulse. As we had expected, all the men wanted to tell us about themselves and their families, and to know all about us. Health Unlimited had given us very clear instructions in how to handle questions about ourselves. Even before the Taliban came to power, Afghanistan was one of the stricter Muslim countries. Men do not usually meet women outside their own household and it is very unusual for women in their thirties, as all three of us were, to be unmarried. Also, knowing that Western women have earned the reputation in some Islamic countries of being 'easy', I had prepared a cover story about being engaged. As luck would have it, my most recent boyfriend had been Egyptian and I had photographs of him to show the Afghans. He wasn't what you would call a strict Muslim, but the Afghans didn't know that, and they were impressed by my claim that we were to be married when I returned home. The only thing that bothered them was that he was clean-shaven: they were convinced that there is something in the Prophet's teachings that says Muslim men must wear beards.

Abdul Wahdood was more interested in my work than in my boyfriend, and was keen to explain Health Unlimited's programme for his area, as well as the political scene there. He was the local Mujahideen commander and the son of Akenzader, the oldest and most revered mullah in the valley. Abdul Wahdood had taken control on the death of his brother, Abdullah, and had been the dominant power in the valley for four years. He was effectively the local head of government and, as long as he supported the work of Health Unlimited, we could count on his protection. Abdul Wahdood had foreseen the legacy of the war with Russia. His valley would only survive with outside aid, and so he contacted the Islamic Aid Health Centre in Quetta which had been set up to give aid to the thousands of Afghan refugees who fled into Pakistan during the war. It was they who had put Abdul Wahdood in touch with Health Unlimited and the charity had now been working in the valley for some five years. The fact that there was a well-established clinic in Daichopan meant that Sarah and Caroline had many advantages over me. They had trained staff to work with and Sarah, having already been out there, spoke the language and was popular with the locals. I began to feel rather isolated and also to worry about the political instability in the area we were going to. Abdul Wahdood could only claim the allegiance of those people affiliated to the Harakat party. This was worrying, as the whole history of the Afghan people was one of wars between tribes, and these tribes were now allied to various political parties. The last thing I wanted was to get caught in the crossfire. My fears were made worse by the news that two French aid workers in Afghanistan had been kidnapped just before our arrival. Only one of them came back alive. I began to have serious doubts about crossing the border at all but Abdul Wahdood assured us that all the troubles were a long way away from his valley and that he could guarantee our safety.

As big a worry as being kidnapped was getting the money we needed sent out from the UK. As the story of ineptitude and bureaucratic bungling unfolded, I was amazed that Sarah and Caroline seemed optimistic about the situation. In fact, it took some six weeks, and a great deal of hard work and foot-slogging, to get any money at all.

Although the clothes I'd turned up in were suitable for Quetta, we would be travelling into Afghanistan disguised as local women, wearing the traditional burkha, which would cover us from head to foot. It is formed from a small cap onto which is stitched a finely pleated fabric reaching right to the floor. A lace panel below the cap allowed limited vision. This was a very safe way for us three women to travel, as no man would dare lift the veil, no matter what his suspicions were: it is forbidden for Afghan men to see the face of any woman who is not a member of their household.

Under our burkhas we would have to wear traditional Afghan dresses and trousers. The dresses had a high neck, no waistline and a hemline below the knees. We were going to wear these to comply with the Muslim dress code and so avoid giving possible offence to the villagers. Given the physical nature of my work, an ample skirt and embroidered bodice with long, full sleeves was hardly ideal.

We had a lot of fun choosing the material for our dresses in the fabric bazaar and chose one of the little shops with an open front and shelves inside stacked with rolls of cloth to make our purchases. The vendor put on quite a show for our benefit. Bale after bale of cloth was unfurled and fanned into the air to land, in multicoloured cascades, at our feet. After we had made our selection, the man balanced on one leg while he deftly rewound the cloth against his other leg. This procedure took an extremely long time. It occurred to me to wonder why we were so concerned about our appearance: it wasn't as if we were going all out to impress the villagers with the way we looked.

My next task was to take myself off to the builder's merchants in search of all the things I needed to take to the valley for my projects. These included galvanised wire, black rubber hosepiping and all manner of bits and pieces. As my Pashtu was still very limited, it was going to be pretty difficult to explain exactly what I wanted. How was I ever going to be able to ask for a tap with a male joint?

At last I was going to be doing something to help the Afghans. During my weeks in Quetta I had begun to get to know these tall, black-bearded characters. Abdul Wahdood, taking his responsibilities so seriously yet maintaining a wry sense of humour. Nur Rajan, quiet and aristocratic-looking in his grey sheepskin hat. The clinic caretaker, Abdul Garni, five foot nothing tall and, with his grey bushy beard, looking for all the world like one of Snow White's dwarfs. Then there was Nur Mohammed, tall and lanky, the joker of the party, nicknamed 'Lunai' (madman) for the crazy impersonations he did. I was getting more excited by the day at the prospect of getting to the valley and starting work.

Sarah had warned me that the clinic at Daichopan was full of mice and this horrified me, as I hated the idea of anything so unhygienic around a clinic. One day I was invited to play volleyball with some of the American aid workers in the grounds of their rather grand villa. However, our game was constantly interrupted by a tiny kitten who wanted to play with the ball. Most cats in places like Pakistan are not domesticated and run wild, but this one seemed very tame. I made a decision to adopt it and, arriving back at our house, announced to Sarah and Caroline that I had 'solved the mice problem!' They thought I was mad. How was I going to transport him on a four-day journey into Afghanistan? What about the heat? What about the cold? How would he survive? What about food? What about water? As they deluged me with questions, I began to wonder if I'd made a terrible mistake. Then the Parker stubbornness took over. 'I'll get a cat basket. It'll be fine, you'll see'.

It was almost time to start off for Afghanistan. I sorted through the few belongings I had brought out with me, leaving a few that I decided I didn't need in the house we had stayed in for the last couple of months. Everything I needed for the next nine months would have to fit into a tin trunk – books, tapes and the three Afghan outfits I would wear. Although it seemed so little compared to the house full of stuff I had left behind in Oxford, there was something invigorating about throwing off the trappings of modern Western life. Then panic set in – about the engineering, about being out of touch with home, about fleas, spiders, lice, worms, stomach trouble, the cold, the heat. I was even panicking about the kitten. Perhaps Sarah and Caroline were right. Would the journey prove too much for him? Would I find food for him? Would he run away en route or be bitten by a scorpion and die?

The lorry carrying most of our goods left a day ahead of us. I must say I was disappointed when I first saw it. I thought it might be one of the brilliantly decorated lorries which we were used to seeing around the streets of Quetta. This one was plain and boring. However, it probably stood a better chance of crossing the border without arousing interest. The tea chests containing medicines went on the lorry first, followed by the tin trunks with our personal belongings in. On top of these we laid our bedding, comprising mattresses and a dozen or so quilts we had bought to protect us from the winter cold, plus a year's supply of toilet paper! Finally, there was the engineering equipment. The lorry set off with some of the Afghans sitting on yet more of our mattresses perched on top of the cab. It was arranged that we would rendezvous with them after we had crossed the border.

Our biggest worry was the money we were carrying, about £25,000 which Abdul Wahdood had managed to get changed into Afghan currency. Much of it was in small denominations and, at the then current rate of exchange, we had about sixteen million afghanis. If we were stopped and searched at the border, which was quite likely, the police would not take kindly to finding us leaving their country with banknotes totalling sixteen million and I had no desire to sample the inside of a Pakistani jail. Then we thought of the all-concealing burkhas. We could stuff all our undergarments with the money and hang bags full of banknotes from cords tied around our waists. We would look extremely fat or heavily pregnant and no policeman would dare lift our veils, no matter how suspicious he was, for fear of offending our menfolk.

Sarah, having travelled to the valley before, warned me that the journey would be long and arduous. She was not exaggerating.

15

The three of us were hustled silently into the back of a taxi with my kitten in a blue plastic picnic basket on my lap. He was fast asleep; I'd dosed him with tranquilliser syrup meant for children. Abdul Wahdood and Nur Rajan sat in front with the driver. Several miles outside Quetta the taxi stopped at a small filling-station. We all got out and were ushered aboard a pick-up truck, having first been warned not to speak a word, as the driver did not know we were foreigners.

No matter how many people a vehicle is designed to carry, Afghans always seem to cram in twice as many. This journey was no exception. There were six of us plus the driver. Abdul Wahdood and Nur Rajan sat in the front, while we three women were squashed in the back with Abdul Garni. I found myself being squeezed against the door with its handle sticking into my hip. The basket with the sleeping kitten was slung unceremoniously onto the pile of luggage behind us. I was very worried about how he would survive the journey, but I was so wedged in that I was never able to turn and see how he was getting on. Visions of the kitten perishing from lack of water, sheer terror or an overdose of tranquilliser filled my mind.

We drove for hour after hour, stopping occasionally at police checkpoints. Each time my heart was in my mouth, but miraculously we were never searched. At lunchtime we stopped and, although we three women were as hungry and thirsty as anyone else, all the men disappeared into a wayside eating-house. Before he joined them, Abdul Wahdood told us that we must wait in the truck, but I feverishly mimed the need for drinking water for the kitten. Shortly he returned with a flask of water, which we eagerly shared with the kitten. Happily I had thought to bring some Crunchie bars with me which slightly alleviated our pangs of hunger. When the men emerged from the eating-house, there was no mention of the possibility that we might also need something to eat.

The whole day was spent inside the hot pick-up truck, and the drive seemed to go on and on, with nothing to see but desert in every direction. We turned off the metalled road and bumped along what was no more than a dirt track. Periodically we stopped for prayers and I grabbed these opportunities to give the kitten some water. By now the effects of the tranquilliser had worn off and I could not get at my bag to give him another dose. However, he seemed very happy and kept bouncing up and down as if he was on springs, so we christened him Zebedee, after the strange character in the BBC children's series, The Magic Roundabout.

It was after dark when we made our final stop of the day. It seemed like the middle of nowhere, but apparently we had successfully crossed the border into Afghanistan. We were escorted into a house that turned out to be very welcoming. We were taken in to what we were told was the guest room. Every Afghan house has such a room built on the outside so that the women of the household cannot be seen by visitors, who are invariably male. Typically for an Afghan house, there was no furniture. There were woven carpets on the floor, while a glowing kerosene lamp hung from one of the walls. The mud on the walls was smoothly plastered with fluted paper fans hanging there like Christmas decorations. Above us the twiggy branches which supported the mud roof showed between the rough wooden rafters. After we had been given tea, we were shown outside to where a spring of clear water glittered in the moonlight. Tactfully our hosts retired to the house so that the three of us could have a much needed wash in private.

When we re-entered the house we were served a splendid potato stew for dinner, after which we spread mattresses and cushions around the wall and settled down for the night, us women at one end of the room and Abdul Wahdood and the men at the other. I slept like a log. The next morning we were given a fine breakfast consisting of tea and kuchi, a delicious sweet brown leavened bread baked by nomads. For security reasons we could not be seen outside, so we spent the morning lazing around and taking tea with the ladies of the house. They were all wearing traditional Afghan dresses with high gathered waists and wide sleeves richly decorated with beads and embroidery, while their hair was firmly plaited with bead ornaments. As soon as they found out that Caroline was a doctor they started to tell her in mime about their various ailments.

To show willing, she examined one of the complaining women thoroughly but could find nothing wrong with her.

It wasn't until after lunch that the lorry with all our provisions and equipment arrived. The rest of the Afghans from Quetta were on board, pleased that they had had no problem with the border police. We got up into the lorry and were greatly relieved when we were told that we wouldn't have to wear our burkhas while on board. The driver was a huge bear of a man with a chubby, smiling face, called Khodai Dahd. Abdul Wahdood sat next to him wearing a bandoleer and nursing his Kalashnikov rifle. Abdul Garni was wedged in between them with his legs wrapped around the gear lever. Sarah, Caroline and I travelled on the shelf at the back of the cab, where long-distance drivers in the UK sometimes sleep. We had piled the last of our mattresses on the shelf and managed to sit there in some comfort, cross-legged leaning against the side of the cab as there wasn't enough room to stretch out. The rest of the Afghans travelled out in the open, perched on top of all our supplies in the back of the truck. The big problem was the dust coming through the open windows in front of us. It was so hot in the truck we would have fried with them closed, but every time we emerged from the cab we were covered from head to foot in fine dust and our hair was caked with the stuff.

Before long the roads began to get steeper and more difficult. At one point, we had to get out and walk, as the lorry was struggling to get up a narrow winding gorge. Eventually we emerged onto a broad plain with a few hills away in the distance. Abdul Wahdood pointed towards these. 'Those are good hills.' 'Why?' I enquired. 'You can hide in them', he replied. What he could not have foreseen was that several of us would almost die in those hills.

Chapter Two

A ll through the journey Abdul Wahdood tried to take care of us, finding food, brewing tea and indicating private places where we could relieve ourselves. On one of these occasions, as soon as we stopped I let Zebedee out for the same purpose and he immediately scampered off. I went after him in hot pursuit, calling for him to come back but, before I had gone more than a few paces, Abdul Wahdood screamed at me to stop. I was in a minefield! Carefully I picked my way back to the truck the way I had come, with Zebedee following. Luckily I arrived there in one piece, but I never again forgot that we were in a country that had spent years at war with the Russian invaders and where fighting between rival factions could flare up any time. On another occasion the driver brought the truck to a screeching halt and grabbed the Kalashnikov rifle from the dashboard. I froze. What terrible peril had he seen up ahead? In fact he just wanted to take a potshot at a magnificent eagle he had spotted perched on a nearby rock. Thankfully the great bird flapped lazily away before the driver could take proper aim.

We reached a metalled road, the Kabul – Kandahar highway, one of the very few proper roads in Afghanistan. However, the journey down it was anything but smooth, as it was pitted with bomb craters and huge grooves cut into the surface by tank tracks. I shuddered each time we passed the burnt-out wreck of a Russian tank. What bridges there had been were all destroyed, and although the rivers were mostly dried up at this time of year, crossing them was slow and tortuous. The truck had to wind its way down one side of the valley and then crawl back up the other. At one point Abdul Wahdood and the driver went into a huddle to discuss our route. Apparently there was fighting around a large town up ahead, so we had to leave the main road and return to the same kind of dirt tracks we had had for most of the journey. I was relieved to find that we were climbing steadily into the 'good for hiding' mountains where the air became very much cooler. My relief was short-lived, for the crumbling mountain roads proved too much for our heavily laden truck. The surface beneath us gave way and we tumbled over and over down the steep mountain slope.

I came to very slowly, uncertain where I was or what had happened. Gradually I realised that I was hanging upside down, with my head resting against something hard and jagged. Reaching out a hand, I felt fur and hardly dared open my eyes in case I discovered a mangled and dying Zebedee. In fact, when I did screw up enough courage to look, two big green eyes stared back at me with a mixture of fear and surprise. He seemed very much alive, with no immediate sign of injury. I on the other hand was in some considerable pain and unable to move. My head was sticking out of one of the truck's broken windows and resting on a sharp rock. That I hadn't smashed my skull in against it was a miracle. Realising that the truck was lying on its side, halfway down a mountain slope, I was seized with panic. What if it should start to roll further down the slope? I had to get out, and quick. But I couldn't move. I was stuck fast, and upside down to boot.

A deathly silence hung over everything and I began to wonder if I was the sole survivor of the crash. I had to get out before the vehicle toppled over again and crushed me to a pulp. Then I heard voices shouting and recognised one of them as Sarah's. I called out as loudly as I could but it hurt like hell to do so; I realised that I had probably broken several ribs. There was a sound of someone scrambling around on the top of the truck, the door above me was prised open and someone grabbed my feet. Slowly and painfully I was hauled upwards in a most undignified manner. At last I emerged on the top of the truck, still confused and semi-conscious. I remember thinking that I must have been the last one to get out of the truck and how lucky I was to be alive. My rescuer carried me away from the wreck, cradling me against his chest as if I were a small and fragile baby. I looked up into the face of Nur Rajan, the tall aristocratic Afghan with the sheepskin hat. As he set me down on the slope, Abdul Wahdood, the young warlord, flashed a broad grin at me. 'You good now?' 'I'm not sure', I replied. 'Everything hurts'. 'Car'nile bad'. He pointed to where, close by, Caroline lay with her eyes closed. Afghans never could pronounce her name. Even from where I was, I could see that she had a serious head wound. I forced myself to my feet and struggled over to her. She had a huge black lump on the side of her head and I had no idea how to help her. I knew little or nothing about medicine and here was the only doctor for hundreds of miles around – unconscious – possibly dying. To my relief, Sarah arrived at my side and took charge. 'Hang on here while I find some of the medical supplies', she said. With that, she was off, scrabbling in the broken packing cases that were strewn across the mountainside. I sat down beside Caroline feeling helpless. Every breath I took was excruciating. Sarah, the heroine of the hour, returned with water, painkillers and antibiotics and spoke reassuringly to Caroline, who had regained consciousness. 'You'll be all right. We'll take care of you.' I was impressed, but I couldn't see how we were going to get out of this mess. Over to my right lay our driver, shaken and badly bruised, while the other Afghans were busily searching the wreckage to see what could be salvaged. Night was approaching and it looked as if we weren't going to be going anywhere in a hurry. No one around us seemed to know what was happening. We sat and waited, as the sky grew darker. There was a lot of excited chattering in Pashtu then, at last, Abdul Wahdood sent two men off to get help. Caroline looked pretty bad to me and, as the temperature began to drop, so did our spirits.

It was completely dark and very cold by the time we saw a set of headlights scything through the night and our rescuers from a nearby village arrived in a pick-up truck. We tucked Caroline up safely in the cab of the vehicle with Sarah nursing her in her arms, while I travelled on the floor in the back, clutching the moneybags and the frightened kitten to me, surrounded by chattering Afghans. It wasn't a long journey to the clinic at Daichopan, perhaps only three quarters of an hour, but it seemed an age, as every bump in the road jarred my broken ribs. What an extraordinary end to our journey this was: me with broken ribs, Caroline with a serious head injury and most of our precious stores and belongings scattered across a mountainside. At least I still had the money!

When we got to Daichopan our first thoughts were for Caroline. Carefully she was lifted from the truck and carried to the clinic. Having a midwife's medical knowledge, Sarah had been able to tend her wound and administer the antibiotics she had salvaged from the wreck. Once we were sure that Caroline was as comfortable as she could be, Sarah and I collapsed onto mattresses on the floor and within seconds were dead to the world.

The following morning I woke early, as is my habit, and tried to get up. This was not easy, as every move was agony, but I was eager to get my first view of the valley. The moment I got outside the building I was spellbound. After days of travelling through barren hills and plains, I was thrilled to see so much water. It was spectacular, the river flowing majestically through the middle of the valley, its course marked by wide gravel beaches and lines of willow trees, their leaves glinting silver in the early morning light. The river was fed by countless little streams and rivulets with soft mossy banks, so that the sound of running water was everywhere. I walked on, across fields and through orchards, hopping over the smallest streams and crossing the wider ones on stepping-stones. Suddenly, through the trees, I caught sight of a village that lay a short distance from the clinic. It looked strangely medieval with houses like small castles built of mud. The early-morning sun threw great shadows across the thick walls and high-set windows, while in the distance the mountains glowed in a rosy light.

The clinic was anything but a castle. It was a primitive affair, long and low, sandwiched between the hillside and a stream, its roof level with the road behind it. Built of the local mud with a flat roof, it had a small mosque at one end, a couple of living-rooms, a kitchen, the so-called 'surgery' and a storeroom. Three more rooms were in process of construction, while a veranda ran along the whole of the front of the building; I soon discovered that this was where the patients queued for treatment. A small bridge crossed a stream and led to a flower garden and a vegetable patch. Beyond these was an orchard; Sarah informed me that this was our toilet! Building a latrine was going to be high on my priority list.

As I approached the clinic after my early-morning walk, the comforting smell of woodsmoke announced that the day there had begun. I found four of the staff sitting chatting on the veranda. Abdul Garni, who had been with us in Quetta, introduced me to the three health workers. Roze Mohammed was tall and handsome, Abdul Wali, despite his good English, seemed rather shy, his heavy, drooping eyelids making him look permanently sleepy. He was shortly to leave for Abqol, a village down river from us, where he would be working in the sub-clinic. Abdul Wahid, the most senior worker, although from quite a lowborn family, had acquired an excellent education and was very experienced. His somewhat haughty and detached air reminded me of a Church of England cleric. He would shortly be running a new clinic in the village of Gazak up in the hills some miles from Daichopan.

Sarah had told me quite a lot about Roze Mohammed and his mother, Kaptara, who was a dai, or birth attendant. She was being taught some rather less primitive techniques, such as the use of a plastic sheet over the mud floor where the baby was birthed and disinfectant for the razor blade used to cut the umbilical cord. Roze Mohammed, who Sarah had grown very close to on her previous stay in Daichopan, was an extraordinary character. Given to violent mood swings, he would be one day wildly boisterous and brimming with confidence and the next depressed and sulky. Nevertheless, he had a good deal of common sense and proved to be an excellent liaison officer between the Afghans and us. He was to be the senior health worker when Abdul Wahid went to Gazak, and later became the most senior worker on the entire project.

Later on that first morning at the clinic, I walked into the kitchen and found Abdul Wali looking at photos of his family. But although he had a camera and was very interested in photography, he was not prepared to share the pictures with me and quickly stuffed them away. Considering how proud most Afghans are of their families, I was surprised. I wondered if it was his natural shyness or, more likely, an example of how closed and private families were in this remote part of the world, with their over-protectiveness of their womenfolk.

In Quetta we had been assured that our house would be ready by the time we reached Daichopan. No such thing. It was still without doors and windows, which could only be bought at the bazaar, a day's journey away. This was a great disappointment to us, as we'd had twelve weeks of sharing a house in Quetta with Joelle, a charming Belgian woman. Nice though she was, all three of us had been looking forward to having our own place. Also, Caroline needed somewhere clean and quiet to rest and recover. As it was, we were crammed into one small, squalid room. Quite apart from the squash, it was not the place for an injured person to recuperate in.

The fourth health worker was a large and rather clumsy Afghan, Mohammed Hussein. He had been assigned to guard the scene of the accident to make sure that none of our supplies or belongings were looted. I was a little disconcerted to hear that this man was subject to 'funny turns'. However, our tin trucks and tea chests, together with much of the supplies, arrived safely. We made no attempt to unpack our own things that day, concentrating on getting the medical supplies into the clinic. To my surprise, Sarah told me to keep an eye on Abdul Garni, as he was considered to be somewhat light-fingered. Apparently things had a habit of going missing when he was around, although no one had been able to pin anything on him. I couldn't understand why he had been one of the people trusted to count the vast sums of cash with us before we smuggled it out of Quetta. Later I grew to understand this kind of ambivalent situation. If an Afghan was told to do one particular thing, he'd do it, and do it correctly. However, if you failed to specify exactly what was desired, and he thought he could get away with doing something else, then he'd do it, because he considered it to be fair game.

For instance, if you told Abdul Garni 'watch those two girls whilst I'm away and, if you lay a finger on either of them, it'll be the worse for you', he wouldn't dream of it. But if on a similar occasion you failed to repeat the injunction, he might well think, 'oh, well, he didn't say anything about not laying a finger on them this time, so this time it's probably all right to . . .' Similarly, when he was counting the money his commander, Abdul Wahdood, was around. Abdul Garni, like everyone else in the valley, worshipped his leader, so he wouldn't have tried anything. At the clinic, however, Abdul Garni was always around the medicines and, unless we kept a very sharp eye on him, he'd try to lift something.

Caroline needed careful nursing and I envied Sarah's obvious skills, wishing I could be of more help. The only useful thing I could do was to carry buckets of water from the stream that ran past the clinic so we could all wash. This job was agony because of my injured ribs, but I soldiered on. There wasn't a hospital for hundreds of miles and, as far as I could gather, no X-ray unit in the whole of Afghanistan. A proper diagnosis of the cause of my pain was impossible, let alone any treatment. Rest might have been good for the healing process, but there was no chance of that. It was a case of grin and bear it.

Washing facilities were basic, although the clinic did boast a hamam, a sort of small bathroom with a cement floor and a tiny door you had to bend very low to get through. The place was just large enough to hold one person and the cylindrical iron stove that heated the water to wash with. A large bucket of water, when heated, was enough for a decent wash, spooning the water over your body with a little aluminium jug called a badini.

On the second day Sarah and I went to see how our new house was progressing. We walked along a track beside the river for about a mile, until we came to the village I'd seen on the first day. This was Bitow, where the warlord Abdul Wahdood lived in a large fortress-like house. Ours was being built near it, on land he owned. It was going to be a great improvement on the clinic, although it was a pity there was no garden.

The flat roof of our house was constructed in the traditional Afghan way with mud plastered on top of carefully laid leafy branches. I was doubtful if this would keep the winter rain out and made a mental note to get some plastic sheeting to cover the whole thing. Like the house where we stayed in Quetta, ours was built around a courtyard, with high walls to stop anyone from seeing the women inside. This suited us fine, as it would enable us to dispense with traditional Muslim clothes while in our own home, without offending anyone. There were six rooms in all, built around the courtyard. Two of the smaller rooms were to be a bathroom and a latrine. However, no one in the valley had any conception of modern plumbing. There was no such thing as connected water, and Abdul Wahdood was the only person in the area to have a well inside his property. Having yet to master the Pashtu language, the only way I could communicate with the builders was by making simple drawings. They had never come across a simple latrine, let alone a flush loo, and there was no way I could have instructed them how to install modern sanitaryware, even if it had been available in Afghanistan.

Using what little of the cement we'd managed to rescue from our crashed truck, I got the men to screed the floor and construct double-offset pit latrine, which sounds complicated but is, in fact, very simple. It has two footplates, like the more primitive French loos, above a chute going out through the wall of the building. Waste is flushed through into one of two pits outside. If one pit is utilised at a time, the latrine is good for many years. By the time the bathroom was finished, my father had managed to send me a camping shower. This was basically a black plastic bag that could be hung from a rafter; attached to it by a length of hose was a showerhead with a little tap. If you filled up the black plastic bag with water and left it out in the sun early in the morning, by lunchtime it would be warm enough to hang up in the bathroom and provide a pleasant shower.

It looked as though there was still a great deal to be done, and the only person who could give us any idea of how long this would take was Abdul Wahdood. Trying to pin him down was like some wild game of hide and seek.

As soon as he arrived in his village he was besieged by visitors anxious to seek his opinion on various important matters. Time and again Sarah and I went to his house. It was like visiting some great Eastern potentate. Passing through huge wooden entrance gates, we crossed the spacious courtyard with guest rooms off it and into the inner sanctum containing the warlord's own quarters. We would hang around hoping to see him but invariably had to give up and return to the clinic. Although we realised that he was the Chief of Police, commander of the local army and the only magistrate in the area, to name but a few of his roles, we really needed to see him and all this hanging around was frustrating. These trips had some side benefits though. Abdul Wahdood's father, Akenzader, was very well-to-do and had three wives. They all had their own quarters in the house, together with some unmarried brothers and the widow of Abdul Wahdood's older brother. For much of the day the women would sit in the main courtyard chatting and sewing. They always seemed to be embroidering something or other: dresses, shawls, wall hangings, or cloths for spreading food out on. These women covered everything in their wonderful traditional embroidery. They always seemed very pleased to see us. I couldn't play much part in the conversation, but Sarah was able to chat away reasonably well, having picked up quite a lot of Pashtu on her previous visits.

It was some time before I got to meet the warlord's father, the great Akenzader, the most powerful man in the district. We had all been working very hard on that particular day, and would have preferred to stay at home for the evening. Caroline was making a miraculous recovery, considering that we were in an area with no sophisticated medical facilities whatsoever. It was evidence of Sarah's skill as a nurse; I was amazed that she found time to tend carefully to Caroline as well as sorting out the clinic medicine store and her other responsibilities as the team leader. We were looking forward to relaxing after another hectic day when Abdul Wali arrived in an agitated state and said, 'Come on.

Come on. The motor is waiting to take you to Abdul Wahdood's for dinner.' His tone made it clear that this was a summons, not an invitation. Caroline, now up and about although not yet fit to work, insisted that she was well enough to accompany us. We piled into the warlord's new Russian jeep to be greeted with excited whoops and cries from the driver. It was Khodai Dahd, the driver of our lorry. The jeep was decorated with plastic flowers, tassels and a large black-and-white photo of Abdullah, Abdul Wahdood's dead brother. As usual, the maximum number of people were crammed into the vehicle – eleven, including ourselves. Off we went, bouncing over the ruts in the road and sliding round the corners. I was just thankful that we weren't going up any steep hills. I had lost faith in Afghan drivers since our horrific accident on the mountain.

On arrival we were shown into the guest room upstairs. It was the first time I had seen a second storey on an Afghan house, and it was unlike any Afghan interior I had seen before. The walls were painted in bright primary colours, which made a nice change from the usual bare mud. And there was a proper wooden ceiling. Abdul Wahid led communal prayers, then Akenzader himself arrived. He was certainly impressive. We had been told that he was 89 years old, which rather shook me, as his son Abdul Wahdood was only in his twenties. I later found out that he had other children as young as seven or eight, and that he was obsessed with his potency, always seeking medicine to help him make more babies! Although he was no great height and somewhat stooped with age, he had an air of supreme authority that I have seldom encountered anywhere. His face was lean and chiselled, with a snow-white beard. Unusually for an Afghan, he wore a white smock, rather like the ones we see English shepherds wearing in period pictures. From the moment he entered the room the atmosphere changed. All the men bowed low to him and the health workers reverentially handed over medicines from the clinic. He studied these with great care, enquiring how efficacious each potion and tablet was.

We three were the only women present; this was obviously an honour for us. The great man appeared to ignore us and, after only a short time, he left the room, everybody remaining standing respectfully until he had gone. The atmosphere became more relaxed and Sarah whispered, "Crikey! That was like meeting the blooming Queen!" The meal that followed was excellent: stew, yoghurt, sweet plums and rice pudding. I was glad that I had at last met the patriarch. On subsequent visits to the house, he would often appear and take my hand in greeting, which surprised me, as he hadn't seemed to notice me at our first meeting. Sarah told me that, even at 89, he had a reputation for being a bit of a one for the ladies and I should watch out where his hands went. There must be something special in the air in that valley!

It began to look as though we would be living in the clinic for some time. Although our room was cramped, I was surprised how easily I took to sharing. I slipped into a routine of going to bed quite soon after the evening meal. The only light to read by was from a couple of hurricane lamps. At first I found their dim flickering very tiring on the eyes, but I soon grew skilled at trimming and adjusting the wicks to obtain a brighter, steadier light. Our evening meals were not to be recommended. I soon stopped wondering what was for dinner: it was always the same – a lump of mutton cut down from a string of dried meat hung along the veranda and stewed in a pressure cooker with a couple of onions and potatoes. The stale bread left over from lunch would be placed in a bowl and the stew poured over it. We would sit on mattresses around a cloth (of varying cleanliness) and each be given a fresh piece of the round, flat bread, which acted as a plate. The large bowl of shalwar, or meat-flavoured bread, was put in the middle of the cloth and we dug in with pieces of bread or just our hands. After the meal, tea would be served in small fluted glasses with little boiled sweets which, although tasteless, provided some sort of relief from the monotony of mutton. Before and after each meal there was a hand-washing ritual. A jug and a bowl would be carried round by one of the health workers and he would pour water over each person's hands as they washed them. Unfortunately most of the local people could not be persuaded to use soap for the hand-washing ritual, so it was no wonder that we three suffered from regular bouts of upset stomachs.

Our meals were prepared by Abdul Hadi, a cousin of Abdul Wahdood. He had a round, smiling face and never wore a turban. This wasn't surprising as the heat in the kitchen soared when he was cooking on his wood-burning stove. But when he poked his head through the small serving hatch to announce that dinner was ready, he always wore a brightly coloured pill-box hat with intricate embroidery on it.

After dinner I would usually chat with the health workers, as they could all speak some English. During these conversations I would also try to pick up a few new words of Pashtu. Having written these down, I would practise them last thing at night and first thing in the morning, at which latter time I would also write up my diary. Before my day began, I would take an early stroll along the river bank, often accompanied by Zebedee. He followed at my heels, like a well-trained dog, and I stopped worrying that he would run away. As we walked, he bounced up and down as if catching imaginary butterflies, and thus continued to live up to his name by emulating the springing character in The Magic Roundabout. I've never met a bouncing cat before or since, so he must be very special.

The butterflies may have been imaginary, but the mice were not. Zebedee proved himself well able to rid the clinic of mice, and the news of his mouse-catching abilities spread far and wide. There were quite a few households that would have liked to borrow him to rid them of their rodents. Afghans do not keep pets and they marvelled at his tameness. Not only did he follow me everywhere, but he always came when I called him. The locals called him 'der special pshay' (the very special cat).

Each morning after breakfast, when the clinic opened for business, a crowd of potential patients would gather on the veranda, spilling over into the orchard close by. There were often a few women whose menfolk had allowed them to attend. Although they did not have to wear the all-enveloping burkha in our valley, they would nevertheless pull their large, brightly coloured scarves over their heads and try to hide themselves away from prying eyes. The health workers would see the patients one at a time, as they were carefully shepherded in and out by Abdul Garni, the clinic's caretaker. Until Caroline was properly recovered, the process was overseen by Sarah. For me it was like stepping back into the Victorian age to learn of the maladies still prevalent in this remote area. These included TB, diphtheria and a host of other diseases hardly ever seen in the Western world.

Although Caroline had gradually recovered from her head injury, she still sported a black eye and it was some time before the swelling to her head disappeared. As soon as she was strong enough to walk to the village she was besieged by local people demanding 'Goli ma ta raka' (Give me pills!). There was always much going on in and around the clinic for, as well as patients coming and going, considerable activity was generated by the construction work on the extension. Also, a constant stream of donkeys struggled past the clinic all day long, carrying heavy sacks of grain to the nearby mill. The one day in the week when there was no activity was Friday, the Muslim holy day. The clinic was closed. The mill was closed. There was nothing for us to do except have a lie-in, and if we were lucky Abdul Garni, the caretaker, would bring us a special breakfast of tea with milk and sometimes some dried fruit. Fresh fruit was unknown in our diet except when occasionally someone would offer us a special gift – an ancient and wrinkled apple! For month after month, with no fresh fruit, salad or greens in our diet, we had to rely on the packets and packets of vitamin tablets we'd brought to keep us healthy. On a working day we would close the clinic for lunch, which usually consisted of scrambled eggs and bread. The Afghan recipe for scrambled eggs is not one that I would recommend. They melt about an inch of oil in the bottom of a pan, then break one egg per person into the hot oil. The whole thing is stirred vigorously into a great greasy mess, which is tipped onto a tin plate so that everyone can dip their bread into it. What with that and the boiled mutton we had for our evening meal our food was very monotonous. I started to dream of tossed green salads, orange juice and grilled steak. The only alternative to the primitive local cuisine was our small stock of chocolate and tinned cheese. As this supply was very limited and we didn't know how long it would have to last, we seldom allowed ourselves to dip into it.

When at last she felt strong enough, Caroline gave the health workers afternoon classes in health for women and children. The information she was passing on to them was of the utmost importance to the well-being of the valley people but the pupils' attention span left much to be desired. All they seemed to want to do was either take a nap or lay out their patous and start to pray. Quite naturally, Caroline was frustrated by this, finding them more like inattentive children than adults anxious to serve their community.

Once the contents of our wrecked lorry had been salvaged and brought to the clinic I discovered that many of my materials were smashed beyond repair. The plastic piping for the ventilation of the latrine was in small pieces. The cement for bridge building was mostly lost, scattered in burst bags on the mountainside, while the tin water-containers were so battered that I thought they would never hold water again. I tried to think positive and concentrate on my main task, building a bridge, although I wasn't at all sure how I was going to do it without the right equipment. The villagers began asking me about the bridge from the moment I arrived and it seemed as if they expected it to be done almost overnight. Abdul Wahdood thought there might be a suitable location just behind his house, but I needed to survey the site thoroughly before I could pass an opinion. For this I was going to need help and no one had yet been assigned the role of my assistant and interpreter. Abdul Wahdood told me that for the time being his second-in-command, Abdul Hamid, would be available to help me. That would have been fine if I ever saw the man. Unfortunately, he seemed to have disappeared and when I enquired where he was the answers from the clinic staff were vague. I began to suspect that he felt the job was beneath him. He had a proud, rather haughty air and this, together with his hooked nose and piercing eyes, put me in mind of the magnificent eagle that our driver had wanted to shoot on our fateful journey into Afghanistan. I wasn't prepared to hang around indefinitely so, after four days of waiting, I set off on my own to explore the area.

On my way to the river to look at the site for the bridge, I met Abdul Garni, the caretaker from the clinic. He was cutting down wood from the trees along the path. I tried to explain where I was off to and, despite his limited English, he seemed to understand. What was more, he indicated that he would like to come with me. I expect he just wanted a break from cutting wood.

When we reached the suggested location for the bridge, I was heartened to note that the river was comparatively narrow at that point, flowing between two high cliffs. I cursed Battle-Axe at Heathrow Airport for forcing me to leave my level and tripod behind. They would have made it easier to measure the distance across the river. Now I could only estimate it by eye. I was only too well aware of the huge responsibility resting on my shoulders. The entire valley was expecting me to build a bridge of enormous strength; the structure that they had in place was of a flimsy, impermanent nature. They had to dismantle it each year before the spring floods arrived, otherwise it would be washed clean away. Without a bridge many of the local people had a four-mile walk to the next point at which they could cross the river. Under these circumstances a visit to the clinic for someone needing serious medical attention could prove impossible. All I had brought with me in the way of building materials was the wire with which I intended to build the huge wire nets called gabions. These could be filled with rocks and placed in the river at strategic points to act as the foundations on which the bridge itself could be supported. All my other projects began to pale into insignificance as I stood and gazed at the swiftly flowing river. It was so beautiful and yet so dangerous. If I built a bridge that failed to withstand the powerful waters swollen by the spring floods, not only would I lose face in the eyes of the whole valley and its warlord, but these poor people would be no better off than when I arrived.

Chapter Three

I needed to figure out just how to build my bridge, so I was glad to gain some thinking time when the chance presented itself for me to visit Gazak. This was an upland area a few miles from Daichopan where my expertise was urgently needed to deal with the disasters that had befallen their irrigation systems. Abdul Hamid was going up there anyway, to visit the newly established clinic, and wanted me to accompany him. He knew that, without a proper flow of life-giving water, the fields in the Gazak area could not produce the cereals and fruit needed for food and for sale to the markets. The area was dying for lack of proper attention to the irrigation systems. We set off with Abdul Wahdood himself flourishing a pistol and wearing a bandoleer of bullets, while Roze Mohammed accompanied us, complete with a Kalashnikov rifle. The third member of the escort was Abdul Hamid, who was unarmed. I naturally thought that we must be setting off into dangerous territory. We were, but the only things my companions shot at the whole time we were away were rocks they picked out for target practice.

Gazak was not only high up, it was also remote. Getting there involved about three hours of steep climbing and, with the memory of our accident still fresh in my mind and my ribs still aching, I didn't enjoy the many narrow mountain paths we had to traverse on the journey. But the trip, although tiring, was very worthwhile, as we went through some wonderful scenery. After crossing the river, we walked through some beautiful orchards, before climbing past a little village in a rocky valley through which a mountain stream bubbled. From here the route got progressively steeper but we took it fairly easily, stopping periodically for the men's favourite game – target practice.

Something happened on the journey that made me suddenly aware of the constant dangers of life in Afghanistan. At one point Roze Mohammed said that we needed to make a detour to the left. This made no sense to me. When I asked him why we couldn't stick to the path that we were on, he replied that it went to a 'very bad' village. When I asked what he meant, he replied, 'Der jang!' I had learnt that 'jang' meant fighting or war, so I accepted that this was an area to be avoided.

There was an interesting follow-up to this incident when, many months later, after news of my work in Daichopan had spread, the people of this 'very bad' village asked for my services to help them with the restoration of their irrigation systems. I was offered safe passage, so of course I went. That's what I had come to this wild, untamed country for – to help the people there build a life after invasion and civil war had torn it apart.

This particular part of Afghanistan has a very complex territorial structure. Daichopan, the valley area under the protection of Abdul Wahdood, who had invited me there courtesy of Health Unlimited, was, if you like, one of many self-governing provinces within the country. On a raised plateau, high above the valley, lay Gazak, towards which I was now wearily climbing. Beyond Gazak lay a vast hinterland known as Harkiran. This was the home of the Hazarahs, a rival tribe to the Pashtuns of Daichopan. Thus, Gazak was a kind of buffer state between the warlord Abdul Wahdood's peaceful valley and the rival tribe occupying Harkiran, who were of Mongol descent rather than Middle Eastern like the Pashtuns. Hence, there were continual border incidents as each tribe made incursions into the other's territory. This was why our sponsor, Abdul Wahdood, was always so hard to get hold of; he spent a great deal of his time up in Gazak, manning the barricades, as it were, against the marauding Hazarahs.

At dusk we stopped for prayers and I heard the men arguing amongst themselves as to which direction Mecca lay in. After this we carried on walking in the dark but, along the way, we seemed to lose Abdul Hamid.

36

He just disappeared into the night without a trace. Nobody seemed unduly worried about this, although I began to wonder how we'd explain to the people of Gazak that we'd mislaid their friend somewhere along the way on a dark mountainside.

Still minus Abdul Hamid, we arrived at a small water- mill. The place was deserted, and when we entered the main building we found a grindstone still with traces of flour on it. The others informed me, in all seriousness, that this was where we were going to spend the night. I looked around the bare stone room in disbelief. We had come on this trip without anything to sleep on, as I had been assured that it was only a few hours' walk up to Gazak. Gradually my companions' dark faces began to break into amused grins. I saw that they were winding me up and sure enough, after a short while, we arrived at Gazak. Waiting there for us was Abdul Hamid, who had run on ahead of us to prepare the way and ensure that we could stay in the house belonging to the family of Abdul Garni, the clinic's caretaker. The Afghans all thought the whole episode was terribly amusing and roared with laughter. I thought it only polite to join in and, as I got to know them better, discovered what great jokers they all were. In a way, it was quite a compliment that they had decided to kid me in this way.

For the first months of my stay in Afghanistan I never quite knew where I was with these smiling charmers. I didn't understand the language and I didn't fully understand why things happened the way they did. I felt like Alice in Wonderland, with everything being topsy-turvy. If I was told to 'go here' or 'do that' I was never sure if it was for my protection or to fleece me of some cash. All the things I used to judge people by simply didn't apply in Afghanistan. Everybody and everything was so different. Were they saying things to be helpful or to get out of doing some work? It was very confusing and it was not easy to help them. Yes, they wanted improvements so that their lives would be healthier and their land more productive and yet they didn't want change if it was going to, in any way, destroy their way of life as it had been for centuries. Change had to be on their terms and it took me some time to work out how best to accommodate their attitude. Unfortunately, a team member who joined us later was unable to accept the prevailing attitude of the local people and all our work nearly went for nothing.

On my arrival in Gazak I was led inside one of the houses to meet the women and children. My grasp of Pashtu was not sufficient to carry on a conversation but everybody chattered away as if I could understand them. I just nodded, smiled and threw in the odd word or two that I'd already mastered. Following dinner I was shown to the room where I was to spend the night. I had to share it with a donkey! As Gazak was high up in the mountains, the nights were very cold there and the thin mattress and cotton quilt that my hosts had provided offered little warmth. I froze. After continually waking up shivering, I decided to try walking around to get my circulation going again. Having paced the donkey room in the pitch dark for what seemed like hours, in the hope of getting warm, I was relieved to hear people moving around and talking outside. Opening the stable door I saw the dawn sky and several of the family drinking tea. They waved to me and I gratefully joined them for a glass. Afghan tea doesn't compare with a nice cappuccino in Starbucks but that morning it was heaven to get some warm liquid inside me.

Later on I was shown the irrigation tunnels called karezes which are driven into the mountainside to reach the water-bearing strata there. They are normally cleared every winter after the rainy season but, during the war with the Russians, they had been very neglected, as most of the men were away fighting. I needed to see exactly what had to be done and estimate the cost so that I could put together a proposal to get some funding. It was sad to see the dried-up irrigation channels and the mouths of the karezes choked with weeds.

As I began to plan how to set about the project, I walked around the beautiful area with its sensational views into the surrounding valleys. I was delighted to think that I would have a really good reason to return here time and again during the coming months. It was an enchanting place, with a small river winding its way through glades of trees that shone with glorious autumn colours. The rocks in this mountainous area were of a pale, pink granite that sprung up in the weirdest of shapes in outcrops dotted across the meadows. I was shown several places in the area that the local people would cultivate if only they could get the water there. I couldn't understand exactly what they were trying to tell me, but they got very excited and obviously thought that I was going to make the whole place fertile again. This was quite a responsibility. On our wander through the fields and woods we came on a man cutting down a poplar tree. My escort chatted to him and then beckoned me over to take a look at the trunk of the tree that was being felled. The woodcutter peeled back the bark to show me a huge beetle. It was about two inches long and had bored huge grooves down the entire length of the tree trunk. 'Chingai' they told me. I had learnt a new Pashtu word and I had also learnt of a new problem. These beetles were slowly destroying the poplar trees that the people here relied on for their building materials. Weakened by the lack of water, more and more trees were falling prey to the beetle. I wished my knowledge of forestry wasn't so sketchy but at least I reckoned I could do something about the lack of water. I longed to help these people get their land fertile again.

At first there was great activity in Gazak, as I toured around trying to take in all the things that needed to be done to get the area fertile and productive again. Then everything ground to a halt. We stopped for a tea break and Abdul Hamid disappeared. He didn't appear again for two days. My decision to visit Gazak had been a rather sudden one and I'd been told that we were going to be staying there just one night. But the Afghans have a different concept of time from us. For instance, I have mentioned that Abdul Wahdood was 24 – because that's what he told me when I first met him. On later occasions he would say that he was 23 or 25. I think they say that they are the age they feel on that particular day. They use the lunar calendar, the Muslim calendar. This has twelve lunar months and a lunar month is just over four weeks long. This is why Ramadan, the ninth month, is eleven days earlier each year. As the months move through the seasons, Afghans do not associate a particular month with a particular season, for example January with winter and April with spring, as we do. Afghans therefore do not celebrate birthdays, although they understand us celebrating them. The women especially have little concept of time, so it's very difficult to judge their age. For them it's very difficult to calculate the weeks, because every day is the same to them – cook, clean, fetch water, take care of the children. Although Friday is the Muslim holy day, in Afghanistan only the men go to the mosque, while the women stay at home and go on working the same as any other day. They do count months, but only in terms of their menstrual cycle. My visit to Gazak was quite early on in my time in Afghanistan and when I was told 'We're just going up there for a day', I took them at their word. Later I learnt that time was much more flexible and relaxed in Afghanistan and the Spanish mañana seems urgent by comparison.

As it turned out, we were up there for four days, much of which I spent sitting around while the men kept going off to conduct other business. Whenever this happened, I would be dumped on a different household. At least this way I got to meet a lot of people and sample how the various families lived. The downside was that I did an awful lot of tea drinking and, if you drink a lot of tea, it has to pass through. Every time I went for a pee, I was accompanied by a bevy of women. As going to the loo involved leaving the house, I assume they were just being protective, but it was off-putting to have an audience every time I wanted to relieve myself.

I regretted not having brought a change of clothes with me and, after four nights without soap to wash with, I could hardly live with myself. Despite this, I felt privileged to have the opportunity to experience life in an Afghan house. I stayed in four different houses altogether. On each occasion the men in my party slept in the guest room, but I as a woman was allowed to sleep with the women and children of the family. Although this gave me a rare insight into Afghan life it was not very restful. The women were great chatterers and were used to sleeping in crowded rooms, so it never occurred to them to lower their voices when

I was trying to get some sleep. There were also numerous babies and, like most babies, they had a habit of crying at night. So, one way and another, I didn't get much sleep during my visit to Gazak. However, it was great to have the opportunity of seeing how the women lived. I had the chance to try my skill at bread making Afghan-style. I'd never used a tandoor oven before: it's really just a hole in the ground with a fire in it. The dough is slapped on the wall of the oven and lifted out as a beautiful, even, round piece of bread. I'll never know how they do it. To the great amusement of the watching women, I dropped my first effort into the fire at the bottom of the oven, while the one that I did manage to rescue was a pathetic moth-eaten affair.

I found it very frustrating not to be able to converse with anyone because of the language barrier. One day, when I was sitting silent in a room full of women, I had an idea. I pointed at the dress one of them was wearing and looked at her enquiringly. She answered me with a word in Pashtu. I tried to repeat it. She said it again and, when I again repeated it, I received a nod of approval. Thus a wonderful game developed in which I would point to an object and one of the women would give me the Pashtu word for it. This was the start of my learning the local language. I decided that, next time I saw Abdul Hamid, I would ask him how to say 'What is this?' In this way I would be able to play the game wherever I went and build up a vocabulary.

Even with the language problem I soon discovered that 'girl talk' is the same the world over. One of the houses we stayed at belonged to Nur Rajan, who had rescued me from the lorry. He had a younger sister who was in her teens and the older women were teasing her about how well her figure was filling out and how she would soon be ready to get married. From the start, Nur Rajan and I seemed to have a special relationship. Unlike most Afghans, he wasn't inhibited about touching a woman. Whenever I was struggling to climb over the rough terrain or in and out of the irrigation works, he was always there to offer me his hand. He was so kind but, unfortunately, he spoke no English. Later on, Sarah told me that he had a bit of a reputation; when he got married, his wife was already heavily pregnant. I wondered how this could have happened, as unmarried men and women were so strictly segregated.

Gazak was really beautiful at that time of the year, with the trees turning every shade of green, yellow, orange and red, while young wheat shoots covered the irrigated fields with a carpet of green. The area's main crop is almonds, as these are easy to transport to market, even from such a remote place. We had arrived at harvest time and everywhere I went I was plied with almonds fresh from the trees. They harvested the nuts by knocking them off the trees with long poles onto sheets spread out beneath.

I found that the local women seemed to enjoy greater freedom here than anywhere else I visited. Very few of the houses had the high protective walls that I had become accustomed to and many of the women worked in the fields alongside their men. To my surprise, one woman even allowed me to take her photograph. Everyone made me welcome, and when they heard that I would do my best to help them they told me that I should have a new name, 'Zurghuna', meaning 'green lady', as they hoped I would make their beautiful landscape green. I felt this rated as highly as 'Palowan' and was determined to live up to my name.

While I was there, I acquired considerable status by repairing the microphone of the local mosque. When I agreed to have a look at it I knew that this was going to be a real test of my skills. I am a water engineer, not an electrician. However, to these people an engineer is an engineer and one who fixes things. I said a silent prayer and decided to start by checking the obvious – the fuse. As luck would have it, I found that this was blown. There was no fuse wire around and I didn't want to lose face, so I wracked my brain for a solution. Then it came to me – I took a piece of silver paper from a pack of water-purifying tablets and twisted it into a makeshift fuse. Not exactly rocket science, but the word spread that the 'engineer lady' could fix anything. Fortunately, as I left soon after, I was spared the ordeal of the whole of Gazak beating a path to my door with every kind of broken-down appliance.

To get funding for the karezes, I would need to get my report back to Quetta as soon as possible. However, working in Gazak wasn't so easy for me. Apart from Abdul Hamid, my interpreter, disappearing, I found myself sent into hiding for an entire day when one of the local mullahs arrived to inspect the new mosque. He did not approve of haraja, that is, foreigners, so I had to be kept out of sight. Then, on the fourth day, Abdul Hamid reappeared and announced that we had to return to Bitow, the medieval-looking village near the clinic. Although I found Gazak enchanting, I was delighted with the prospect of a good wash and a change of clothes.

The trip back from Gazak was mostly down-hill. As this required considerably less effort than the journey up, I was able to spend time drinking in the wonder of the Afghan scenery. I rejoiced that my work was going to involve so much travelling in this amazing country. It was the sort of fairytale land I'd dreamed about as a little girl. But I knew that the romance was likely to wear thin when the heavy winter snows arrived and trapped us in the valley for months on end. I could also imagine that, in the spring, the rain would come through the ceiling and I had been warned that, in the summer, the ghastly spiders that live in the twigs that make up the roofs of the houses would chew bits out of us. They were hibernating at present, but at their most active they lower themselves on their thread and inject a form of anaesthetic into whatever part of the body is exposed, usually the face, and then proceed to eat it. The anaesthetic stops the wound from healing. Sarah said that the worst wounds she ever had to deal with were spider bites. Despite all this, I was glad I'd come. The country was like nowhere I'd ever been and the people and their culture were fascinating.

As soon as I got back to the clinic I started to compose the report that would support my application for funding the work at Gazak. Getting funding was easier said than done. I could hardly forget the merry-go-round of trying to find the money to finance this year's projects while we were still in Pakistan. Back then I knew nothing about the funding of Health Unlimited, which was dependent for its finance on the larger agencies, or the extent of the financial problems facing the Afghan project. The procedure was that we submitted plans for our projects with financial estimates to a specific agency and then, if they liked the idea, they provided the money. The estimate for my particular year was based on the previous year's funding and had been submitted some time before I arrived on the scene. We were supposed to receive money from the World Health Organisation (WHO) and the UK Overseas Development Agency (ODA) (now the Department for International Development, DFID), but a much more complex situation was unfolding before me.

The team previous to mine had agreed with Abdul Wahdood that they would pay for him to build two sub-clinics and a house for the team. He had gone ahead and started that work in good faith and had accumulated bills of £2,000 which, in his part of the world at that time, would have been the equivalent of untold thousands of pounds in the UK. Until we came up with the money, he could not go back to Daichopan, as all the local builders there were awaiting payment. So he was exiled in Quetta for three months while we struggled to get the money together.

Part of the problem was international politics. The World Health Organisation obtained its funds from Japan, but the donors were getting cold feet about putting money into Afghanistan. They'd heard about the conflict between the different Mujahideen factions after the Russians left, and we had to assure them somehow that we would not be affected. Contrary to what the Western press was publishing, there was no general antagonism towards aid from the outside world. Anyway, the areas where the fighting was taking place were a long way from our valley, or so we were assured.

Another major problem was disorganisation. We asked the ODA for their contribution on several occasions; they kept assuring us that it had already been sent out to Pakistan, but it always transpired that the money they were talking about was designated for other projects. Eventually we discovered to our horror that they had lost that year's application, and we had to submit it again. This was a mere nothing compared to the difficulties we experienced with Health Unlimited. The director had just resigned and the desk officer who had interviewed me in London had gone to another job. During our first few weeks in Pakistan the London office was run by a nurse who had been on the previous team in Daichopan and was trying to cope with a job about which she knew almost nothing. I saw no alternative but to go out and try to raise the money myself and managed to get £1,000 for my projects from Oxfam. I was able to get this fairly quickly because a local Oxfam country manager can sign for this sum without having to get UK authorisation. I believe that, as the situation was so critical, Health Unlimited took money out of their reserve funds, but only the bare minimum that was needed for us to go into Afghanistan. This was on the understanding that money would be forthcoming from the Overseas Development Agency to make up for this.

Before getting funds I put together a detailed proposal for my main areas of interest, including the riverbank protection scheme and the building of the new bridge which would require that we make gabions as supports for the bridge, which had previously always been washed away in the spring floods. To improve the drinking-water and sanitation I planned to build pit latrines for each of the three clinics, the school and the house, and install sand filters at each of the sites. Altogether I reckoned I would need about £5,000. If I failed to get the money, I would stay in Daichopan until December, do what surveying I could and prepare a detailed report and budget. At least, if I submitted this to Health Unlimited, they might just get their act together financially and send another engineer out the following year to get the work done.

Quitting Afghanistan in December would leave me with seven months to fill in. Thames Water weren't expecting me back until July and I had let my house in Oxford for a full year. Maybe I could get some kind of job in Quetta. I'd made useful contacts at an engineering company there. They were working on irrigation schemes in the area and had difficulty finding people to work in Quetta – it was considered a hardship post! With hindsight I can say that Quetta was the height of luxury compared to life in Daichopan. I mean, they had flush toilets and proper gas cookers in Quetta. The money came through in the end, I'm happy to say, so my contingency planning was not required after all.

My stay in Quetta convinced me that the expatriate life was not for me. There were several hundred there, all trying to maintain a Western lifestyle. This small, bigoted community had its own hierarchy. At the top of the pile were the UN staff and employees of commercial companies. They earned very good money and had a comfortable lifestyle with large houses and servants. They usually had access to alcohol through UN or delegation stores, had Western supplies flown in and were chauffeur-driven in top-of-the-range four-wheel-drive vehicles. Then there were the people who worked for organisations like Oxfam, Médecins sans Frontières and Save the Children Fund. They were reasonably well paid but often several of them would share a house. They had a pleasant enough time, although alcohol was a rare treat. The house we were staying in belonged to the Belgian midwife, Joelle Dubois. She was friendly and chatty and quite happy to have other people living in her house. Western goodies like fresh coffee and dried herbs were in limited supply in Quetta but, when she could get them, Joelle was happy to share these with us. She too had worked in Afghanistan with Health Unlimited and so was well aware of the charity's lack of proper organisation. Like all the houses in Quetta hers was enclosed by a high wall with large iron gates in it. This was partly tradition, so men could not see the women inside, but it was also necessary because of the high crime rate. Inside the walled area was a small courtyard with an ornate terrazzo floor and several blue-painted wicker chairs. When we first arrived there, we used to enjoy sitting outside, but eventually something, the sewers, or the cows opposite, got too smelly to bear, and we had to stay indoors.

Writing a report on the situation in the Gazak was anything but easy. For instance, there was the question of exactly how many villages there were in the area. Abdul Wahdood said 14 and Roze Mohammed thought 15. When I asked them to name them all it came to 17, but then I discovered that some of the names they had given me included more than one village. I also had to work out how many men I needed for the work and how long it would take. How long is a piece of string? No one there had ever done this kind of work and I was used to the regimentation and efficiency of Thames Water back in the UK. When I'd worked everything out, mostly by guestimates, I had to type it up, not one of my top skills. It took me about two weeks in all to get it finished and by this time I was desperate for some fresh air and exercise. As I needed a plan of the area around the clinic to help design the bridge and none existed, I decided to draw one myself.

All I had with me for this purpose was my pedometer, for measuring distances by walking, and my compass, so I knew which way I was walking. I had a little portable drawing-board and getting all the information onto this was a laborious business. I spent day after day tramping over fields, pushing through hedges and wading across streams. Gradually the picture of the area began to come together and, by the time I had finished, I was a lot fitter than when I'd arrived in the valley. Before long I was doing twenty-five miles a day on foot. Back in the UK, I had struggled to complete a twelve-mile sponsored walk.

During my tour of the area I often came across small boys playing and they would always call out the same thing to me, 'Akaz waka', which I discovered meant 'Take a photo'. All Afghan males love having their photo taken! The children I met on my travels around the area were fascinated by the ocarina that I carried around my neck. This tiny wind instrument was made of pottery and had been a going-away present from my sister when I left the UK. It had a very strange shape and, with only four finger holes, it wasn't easy to play. It took me weeks to master 'Happy Birthday' for Caroline's celebration. Frankly, it wasn't much of a substitute for my double bass, but I used to make up little tunes which the children took a delight in singing and dancing to. I must have looked like the Pied Piper, as I wandered across the rugged landscape with bunches of kids following my weird music.

Afghanistan is a country rich in all forms of culture, but the travelling musicians seldom reached our isolated valley, so the only music-making we came across was from local women beating drums and singing at special celebrations. Caroline told me about a mysterious shepherd boy who she had once seen playing a version of Pan's pipes. Sadly, I could never find him; I would have loved to try his pipes.

I'd made sure to bring my Walkman with me from England – another treasured possession I would not wish to be parted from. I took a batch of my favourite tapes, Elgar, Dvorák, Duke Ellington and many others. A piece of music that always conjures up the spirit of Afghanistan and my time there is Dire Straits' song 'Brothers in arms'. The words 'Those mist-covered mountains are home to me now' seemed so appropriate. The same tape had a bouncy number called 'The Walk'. It was good for getting me up steep mountain paths and I adopted it as my 'walking to Gazak' music.

One day, while I was tramping around designing the map, I met Abdul Wahdood's youngest brother, who beckoned me to follow him. He took me up onto the flat roof of his house which had a glorious view of the surrounding area, and I learnt that the patriarch, Akenzader, would spend much of his time up there, surveying his land. In the storerooms just below were trunks holding the equipment and personal effects that earlier teams had left behind. It was a wonderful surprise to discover that the previous team had left some music tapes when they went back to the UK; I had got bored with the tapes I'd brought out.

It became obvious to me that I had need of a good assistant, but such a person was not easy to come by. When I approached Abdul Wahdood he produced a man who he said would 'protect' me. I hadn't really been looking for a bodyguard. In any case, Mullah Ahmed Zai didn't look capable of 'protecting' anyone. He was several inches shorter than me. He looked aged and wizened, with a straggly grey beard, crooked yellow teeth and a pronounced limp. It was probably some considerable time since he had been acquainted with soap and water. I was told that he had studied English with previous project managers, but he must have been a very poor student; the only phrase he could say was, 'I have a father and a mother'. Apart from his inability to converse with me, he didn't look like the kind of man to leap into a river in order to hold a tape measure for me, never mind defend me against roaming wolf packs. I couldn't be too rude about the man as he was Abdul Wahdood's uncle. I voiced my concerns as politely as I could to Abdul Wahdood, who came up with a much better candidate, a young man of about eighteen who was very keen to work with me and expressed an interest in 'sums'. Sadly, his father wouldn't let him take the job, insisting that he needed him to work on the family's land.

I had hoped that Abdul Hamid would be available to help me and I couldn't understand why this wasn't possible. Eventually I found out that he resented Roze Mohammed being given the position of Senior Health Worker. Sarah told me that, although he was very able, Abdul Hamid was not as trustworthy as Roze Mohammed. Time was running out and I still had no one to assist me. Concerned for my safety, Abdul Wahdood did not want me to go beyond the village on my own. It looked as though I'd spend the rest of my time in Afghanistan sitting in the clinic and accomplishing nothing.

Chapter Four

One day in early October we were caught off guard by the arrival of someone completely unexpected. Caroline was still in bed and I was finishing my breakfast when an English voice called out 'Hello there!' I swung round to see a dishevelled, bearded character in the doorway. 'I'm John Gibb-Smith from Leprosy Control', he said. It turned out that he'd been driving since four in the morning and was just about deadbeat. There was fighting between rival factions in the area where he was working and he had reluctantly decided to make his escape in the middle of the night, accompanied in his battered old van by three loyal Afghans. After a meal and a well-earned rest, John and his companions climbed back into their van and headed off to Quetta, where he hoped his wife would be waiting for him. I thought it ridiculous that such a useful and well-intentioned person should be forced to leave Afghanistan, just because of stupid local feuds and squabbles. It was not until I had lived in the valley for some time that I understood the Afghan moral code and its ramifications. An insult has to be avenged, particularly an insult to a woman. Vengeance usually takes the form of killing or serious wounding, and from these incidents arise the localised feuds that plague the country. Vengeance goes from generation to generation. It isn't just a case of he kills your brother, so you kill his – it goes on indefinitely. That explained why no one went near the 'very bad village in Gazak': it was the result of a particular feud that had gone on for generations.

Shortly after I had arrived in Daichopan, Abdul Wali had gone to Abqol to work in the sub-clinic there. From the moment of his arrival he had been sending back a stream of pathetic letters addressed to Caroline. They complained of the conditions he had to live and work under, including a leaking roof and nothing proper to sleep on. Caroline had been up there and told me the area was well worth a visit. She didn't want to go herself, partly because she suspected that Abdul Wali's letters of misery were designed to get her there. When I first arrived I had noticed him trailing around after her with sad eyes and a hangdog look. It was obvious that he had a crush on her. Sarah reckoned that the other reason he wrote to Caroline was because he thought she was a softer touch. He was always trying, without much success, to get more money out of Sarah. It wasn't that she was hard-hearted; we just didn't have any cash to give. For myself, I wanted to go to Abqol because I'd heard that the area was suffering from severe flooding and soil erosion and I was eager to see what I could do to help. I was also keen to grab any chance to visit other parts of the valley.

Having learnt my lesson on the trip to Gazak, I was determined to be prepared this time. Not having done much walking until my trip to Afghanistan, I crammed all manner of things into a backpack, enough for the week I was expecting to be away. But I could hardly lift it, let alone carry it for a whole day's hike. I clearly had to reduce my burden considerably. I was to be accompanied by Khodai Mir, the young man who was 'good at sums', whose father had been persuaded to release him. As there was no question of travelling outside our valley unarmed, a search was mounted for a weapon; it produced a spare Kalashnikov rifle. We set off, just the two of us, early in the morning. We hadn't been going for more than a quarter of an hour before we stopped at the village of Tsangtmor. This was where Khodai Mir lived and he wanted us to meet his family.

The house was jampacked with people. I was introduced to various family members and their children before meeting the young man's pretty, smiling wife. I was somewhat taken aback to find that the tall, gangly youth was married, forgetting for the moment that many Afghans embark upon this life partnership at a very early age, with girls being married at 14 or 15. I found Khodai Mir's father seated at a treadle sewing-machine, making himself a long shirt, the top part of the traditional shalwa kameez worn by all Afghan men in the area. He pedalled away furiously, lit by the sun that shafted in through a small window above his head. While he worked, we all drank tea and ate bread dipped into goat butter. For some reason it tasted like Christmas cake!

It was the middle of the morning before we set off again, down a narrow ravine with dramatic overhanging cliffs. The sun caught the pale pink granite in these, making the crystals in the rock glitter and sparkle.

In places there was hardly room to walk between the river that whirled and rippled beside us and the vertical face of the gorge. Suddenly Khodai Mir disappeared round a huge outcrop of rock only to reappear above me. It was difficult to see how he'd done this, and following him was tricky with a rucksack on my back and wearing a voluminous dress. It was worth the effort for it gave us an excellent view beyond the end of the gorge to the next part of the valley, filled with the familiar mud houses.

We emerged from the gorge into narrow fields of almond trees and wheatfields running alongside the river, whose small streams served to water them. The going through the gorge had been tough and Khodai Mir, with some reluctance, had been persuaded to carry my backpack for a while. After half an hour he abruptly handed it back to me, complaining that it was too heavy for him. I wondered if I had lumbered myself with the least macho man in the valley. On and on we walked, hopping over the small streams, and wobbling along the narrow paths beside the river bank. Gradually the valley opened out before us, as the river swept round a sharp bend with high cliffs on either side. Pyramids of tree trunks rested against the cliffs, presumably to protect them from further erosion by the river. Looking at the gently flowing water, I marvelled that, as it leapt and danced through the gravel shoals, it was capable of smoothing pebbles and undermining cliffs. Some of the land close to the river had been painstakingly reclaimed by the building of small embankments with willow cuttings planted into them. Once enough earth had been deposited rice could be sown in the fields.

We walked quickly through the next village, armed with stones to throw at unfriendly dogs. I had learnt that most dogs in Afghanistan are unfriendly. They are deliberately bred to be ferocious and defend their territory. When strangers pass, they tear out barking and growling in a frightening manner. Much as I hate throwing stones at dogs, I'd rather do that than receive a rabid bite.

Beyond the village, the fields got smaller and smaller and the valley started to close in on us again, with granite cliffs towering up on either side. My feet were aching and the rucksack felt as if it was full of lead weights. I'd always avoided hikes and sponsored walks so, by the time Khodai Mir suggested we stop for tea, I felt I'd never walked so far in all my life. We arrived at a large mud house and were shown into the guest room. The walls were painted bright turquoise; I wondered how they managed to get the paint to stick to the bare mud. Posters of dramatic alpine scenes were stuck on the wall and, around the top of the room, a frieze in red and white added a bizarre effect. Exhausted, I collapsed onto one of the mattresses on the floor. No sooner had I done this than the owner of the house rushed in, crossed over to me and wrenched open his mouth to display some very unsightly teeth. I was completely taken aback until Khodai Mir explained that the man thought I was a dentist and wanted his teeth checked. After much chattering and hand-waving he was finally convinced and left the room dejectedly. He returned shortly afterwards with a pot full of tea and a tray of glasses. I was so tired and thirsty that the first few glassfuls went down almost without touching my throat. For once I was glad of the thick layer of sugar poured into the bottom of my glass. Feeling better, I curled up on the mattress and could happily have rested there all day, but Khodai Mir said we had to be on our way so I heaved on my rucksack and we set off again.

We trudged on and on and only the beauty of the scenery kept me going as, round each bend in the river, yet more wonderful vistas unfolded. The granite of the cliffs shone even pinker as the river sparkled and danced beneath them. It was difficult to imagine that this beautiful country was caught up in a brutal civil war. It had been a land at war with itself and numerous invaders since its history began. Dusk was already making the path more difficult and dangerous as we rounded a bend and saw a small, low building tucked into the hillside. It was just like a smaller version of the clinic at Bitow, so I guessed that we had at last arrived, even before Khodai Mir walked confidently up to the door and tried it. My heart sank when he turned to announce that it was locked. This didn't seem to worry him, as he said Abdul Wali was probably at his parents' house just round the corner. Thankfully, it really was very close and, as we approached, Abdul Wali and his brother, Mohammed Khan, rushed out to explain that this was a very special day; they were celebrating the engagement of their niece, Sunsullah. When I enquired how old she was, I was told that she was six. I was only momentarily surprised as, in Afghanistan, it is normal for children to be betrothed as young as this. In most cases, it is regarded merely as a business arrangement. I was fascinated to find out more about engagement customs/practices and was able to chat to Abdul Wali, as he spoke English quite well. He said he would be getting engaged soon as well, to a girl whose family lived near his. He was very pleased as they had played together when they were both small children.

A special meal had been prepared to celebrate Sunsullah's engagement. I was introduced to everyone as the 'English engineer' who was here to bring help to the region – quite something to live up to. I should have counted myself lucky to have arrived on such a special day but, frankly, I was too exhausted to be much interested in the joyful proceedings. I couldn't follow all the conversation, so I sat quietly in a corner while dish after dish of delights was produced for the guests who now filled the room. As usual we sat on mattresses and ate off round cloths spread out over the carpet. Eventually Khodai Mir, perhaps sensing how tired I was, whispered that we should go back to the clinic. Abdul Wali soon joined us there and lit a fire which filled the room with the aromatic mountain wood's heavy scent. I went outside for a quick wash in the stream and, on my return, found large quilts unrolled on top of the mattresses. I had grown accustomed to the unisex sleeping arrangements that I encountered on my travels, and I never at any time felt at risk while under the protection of these kind souls.

Unfortunately, even my thick quilt was not enough to keep out the cold, so I sat by the still-burning wood fire to warm myself. The clinic chowkidar, or caretaker, arrived at 6.30 and we had the usual breakfast of tea and bread. The engagement celebrations were still in full swing and, feeling a little more rested, I was able to take in my surroundings. Abdul Wali's family lived in a sprawl of mud buildings around a courtyard with a huge walnut tree growing in the middle. His two married brothers had their own accommodation in the complex. His parents' house consisted of an outer building full of sheep and hens where the cooking was done when the weather was bad, and a cosy inner room that boasted a rough wooden bed similar to Indian charpoys, as well as the usual tin trunks and mattresses.

We visited the room where Abdul Wali's elder brother, Karim Dahd, resided. Its walls were covered with pages from photographic magazines which a previous expat team member had sent to Abdul Wali. The older brother had decided that he wanted these for room decoration and the younger man had no say in the matter. I didn't take to Karim Dahd, a large man with a forceful personality. My feeling was that even if his age hadn't given him precedence over his younger brother, he would still have snatched whatever he wanted for himself. Perhaps having such an overbearing elder brother partly explained Abdul Wali's hangdog expression. I felt sorry that we Englishwomen had been so dismissive of him.

The celebrations turned out to consist of yet more eating. I watched the women of the house working with just a few large pots and pans to produce another feast with stews, boiled meat, the ubiquitous shalwar, and stewed dried plums and yoghurt. As a non-Muslim I was not allowed to stay in the room for the blessing of the betrothed couple so I waited outside in the yard where children were rushing around in the dust and dirt. The engaged couple were no older than these children.

Once the guests had left we went back to work. That afternoon, I met with representatives from seven surrounding villages to establish how I might help them. Even with Abdul Wali acting as interpreter, it was hard work trying to make out exactly what it was they needed. Dinner that evening was in stark contrast to the rich meals I'd experienced over the previous two days, just plain boiled rice sprinkled with a little oil and sugar. I went to bed early but was prevented from getting a good night's sleep by some unexpected visitors – the fleas had discovered me.

I tossed and turned and scratched all night, getting up extra early to avoid the little devils. When I explained what had happened, everyone was sympathetic and made a great fuss of me. Someone organised warm water for me to wash in and there was leavened bread. This treat was kuchi, or nomad bread, and it was delicious. After this special breakfast, I went walkabout with my assistant, Khodai Mir. The idea was to collect as much information as I could with a view to making a map of the area. We had only been going for about an hour, when my companion sat down on a rock and announced that it was time to go back to the sub-clinic. I put him straight but, as the day wore on, he became more and more disgruntled. By the time we arrived back in the late afternoon, I had a near-mutiny on my hands. I was tired myself by then, but I couldn't resist when Abdul Wali and Mohammed Khan offered to take me up the mountain to get a good view of the river and the problems caused by its flooding. I amazed myself at how high I managed to climb, slipping and scrambling most of the way and sometimes hauled up bodily by the men. It was well worth it to get such a breathtaking view of the valley. The river snaked from side to side far beneath us and the two brothers pointed out the gravel shoals that were part of their father's land and which had been good farmland until the flood washed the soil away.

Over the next few days I had more meetings with various people in the area to enable me to put together a report about work required in the area to reduce flooding and improve irrigation. One individual was quite different from the rest. He was clean-shaven, which was very unusual in those parts, and he wore a huge fawn-coloured patou or woollen shawl and a brightly coloured pillbox hat. His demeanour was extremely arrogant; he was an official of the Jemiad party and was known as Mullah Mungal. His party came principally from southern Afghanistan. All the people in this area were part of the Kaka tribe, a subdivision of the Pashtun race. A tribe was very different from a political party, similar to Scotland where you might be members of the McDonald clan but could belong to different political parties. All the Pashtuns were eventually united by the Taliban.

Mullah Mungal had been educated in Kabul and took great delight in speaking to me in Arabic. I couldn't understand why until Abdul Wali told me that he had explained to this man that I was engaged to an Egyptian. I was glad that I had made up the story about my forthcoming marriage to Yasser. The word always seemed to spread before me and it undoubtedly made most of the Muslims feel happier in my presence. It was almost true as Yasser had asked me to marry him and I'd only broken the relationship off a year before.

The man in the pillbox hat invited me to go to his village the next day to see the problems they were facing, but this idea seemed to make Abdul Wali nervous. Later on he suggested that I take Karim Dahd with me, as there could be trouble in the village. Pillbox and his people owed no allegiance to Abdul Wahdood. In fact Abdul Wali and his family were the only people in the area who were followers of Abdul Wahdood. I was beginning to realise how risky and unpredictable travel in Afghanistan could be. The country was like a series of small principalities, each one the province of a fierce warlord. In addition, different tribes and political parties vied for power in their area. Abdul Wali was not convinced that Khodai Mir, my so-called assistant, would be any use in a tight spot, even with a Kalashnikov rifle, so we agreed that I would be better off taking Karim Dahd with me.

I was still finding it hard to get a decent night's sleep, as the fleas refused to leave me alone. Each morning I woke up covered in bites and sores where I'd been desperately scratching myself all night long. I was not on top form and did not feel fit to venture bravely into hostile territory. The wind was bitterly cold but fortunately I had thought to pack my long johns. Putting them on without exposing myself in public involved some crafty acrobatics under my quilt. I could never understand how the Afghans were able to withstand the cold: their only clothing was a shawl, or patous, and under this a thin cotton shalwa kameez, plus flimsy rubber shoes and no socks.

Next day we made our way to the village we had been invited to visit. Our hosts led us up the mountain so that I could see how a stream formed by digging into water-bearing rock disappeared into the gravelly ground. They told me that they needed cement to build a course for the water so that, instead of losing it, they could guide it down to irrigate their fields on the lower slopes. We were invited to take tea with them back at their village; Karim Dahd indicated that it would be unwise to refuse their hospitality. Our hosts brought out a magnificent water-pipe. Karim Dahd puffed away at it contentedly, and I wondered if he had been only too happy to stop off for tea, anticipating an invitation to smoke the hookah-like pipe.

Tea and water-pipe finished, we set off again, this time up to the riverbank where Karim Dahd explained that we needed to cross over to see some work on the other side. I was not looking forward to a knee-deep paddle in the icy river, but I was rescued from this fate when a man rode up on a magnificent horse with embroidered saddle clothes and bridle, looking as if he'd just stepped out of the Arabian Nights. Karim Dahd and the rider quickly consulted and the man dismounted, handing the reins to Karim Dahd, who leapt into the saddle with great agility and indicated that I should jump up behind. My attempt was less elegant, but I managed to scramble up. I must have looked incongruous in my shawl and baggy dress, but at least my green wellies were appropriate and I was glad of them as the horse bucked and splashed through the water. Karim Dahd let me dismount, equally inelegantly, and cantered back to get the owner, whose athletic vault behind the rider showed me how it should have been done. Khodai Mir plodded across on a moth-eaten donkey, which seemed rather appropriate! On the far side we saw soil erosion and dried-up irrigation channels, but I was also shown two diesel pumps chugging away in a sump which was fed water from the river via a tunnel dug through into the cliff which formed the river bank. The country was such a collection of anomalies, ancient farming practices alongside Walkmans, marriage arrangements of a kind that died out centuries ago in the West, mixed with modern irrigation techniques.

I returned to the clinic with the undeserved status of a heroine who galloped across the river on horseback and ventured into hostile territory. Abdul Wali's nephews and nieces followed me around calling me by my Afghan name 'Zurghuna'. They were an appealing group with huge brown eyes and coffee-coloured skin, sporting brightly coloured waistcoats and dresses which were covered with intricate embroidery. To entertain them I played 'ring a ring a roses' with them and taught them 'Ging Gang Gooley'; although they never managed most of the words, they soon caught on to the 'oompahs'. It wasn't long before I acquired an entourage almost everywhere I went, shouting 'Oompah, oompah' and asking for a song.

Khodai Mir continued to be an unwilling assistant. He lagged behind when I was out surveying and talked over people's answers when I was carrying out my surveys. The only thing he would do willingly was cook. His efforts were quite edible, although Abdul Wali said that he had tried him out as a cook at the main clinic but dismissed him after everyone became ill. Abdul Wali got just as exasperated as I did and named him Cecil, after a caterpillar in a poem which Caroline had taught him. Cecil the caterpillar had eaten and eaten until he was sick, which seemed appropriate. Abdul Wali took great delight in calling Khodai Mir 'Cecil' behind his back; the name did rather suit him. Khodai Mir eventually got wind of his nickname, but as he didn't know the poem or anything about the name, he remained blissfully unaware of the private joke between Abdul Wali and myself.

Most of the evenings passed quietly. If I was in the main house I would sing songs to everyone and teach Abdul Wali's sisters some folk

60

dances. The Afghans loved even the simplest songs and dances and would request 'Ten Green Bottles' over and over again. They also liked my song-and-dance version of 'The Good Ship Lollipop', although it lacked something without tap shoes. Abdul Wali's favourite pastime was Ludo; I lost count of the number of games I played with him, Khodai Mir and Mohammed Khan, crouched beside the stove in the flickering light of a hurricane lamp.

The penultimate night brought the promised celebrations for Abdul Wali's engagement. Before we set off for his fiancée's house I had a very welcome shower or hamam. The bathroom was tiny and the stove was stoked up, with the tank above full of steaming water. There were two buckets full of cold water on the floor, which I could hardly stand on, as the stones were heated by a vent running from the stove. I passed my clothes out to Karim Dahd's wife and was handed one of his outfits to wear whilst my clothes were washed and dried. I wished I could wear the men's shalwa kameez all the time. It was made of soft cotton and the long shirt was practical and comfortable, a welcome relief after the swathes of material in the full-skirted dresses I had to wear. I emerged from the hamam feeling like a new woman. As I was beginning to have a firmer grasp of the language, I was pleased to be able to sit and chat to the women in the house while my clothes steamed over the stove. When they were dry enough to put on, I changed into them and set off for the next village with Abdul Wali, his father and brothers, and Khodai Mir. Of course, the women were not allowed to come but they didn't seem to mind. They took it for granted, and expressed surprise when I asked them if they were sorry not to go.

Abdul Wali's fiancée lived in a large mud-walled house which looked like a fortress. It had a huge gate with a room over it, and as we passed through the gate I felt what I thought were a few drops of rain on my head, which was strange as the weather looked fine. The rest of our party were laughing and pointing up at the gatehouse. Abdul Wali explained that it was traditional to play jokes on the prospective fiancé at these celebrations, such as surreptitiously sewing his clothes to the mattress as he ate or hiding his shoes. This time the family had emptied buckets of water over us as we entered.

We were led into a very splendid guest room with a wood-panelled ceiling. 'That would keep the spiders at bay', I thought. Guests arrived, including the leader of the Jemiad party who seemed to rule the roost and monopolised the conversation. Abdul Wali whispered odd snatches of translation for me and this, with my rapidly improving Pashtu, helped me catch the gist of what was being said. It seemed very complimentary about the work that Health Unlimited had done in the past and what they hoped it would do in the future. When the food arrived, everyone kept passing me small pieces of chicken as presents, or 'swammies' as they are called in Pashtu. It was a mark of great favour and of course I couldn't refuse, though I would rather have had more yoghurt and plums! Tea took so long to arrive that I was almost asleep. Eventually we were led into the house and given more tea, and then at last our beds were made up and I could get some sleep with – oh bliss – no fleas.

The next morning we were woken up early but Abdul Wali soon disappeared with Khodai Mir. I was brought tea and boiled sweets and left on my own. Children came and went, looking at me with curiosity and asking me questions. In turn I asked where everyone was and if I could join them. As I understood it, this was not acceptable, although my Pashtu was too limited to fathom out why. Perhaps there was another religious ceremony. If that was the case I was sorry I could not see it, but non-Muslims were not welcome at any religious occasion. So I sat and waited and wished I had something to read, other than my list of Pashtu vocabulary. A couple of small children came in and I showed them my dictaphone. One of them recited what I recognised as the Islamic prayers, which I had certainly not expected. Then some of the women came in and asked me all the usual questions. Was I married? Did I have a mother and a father? I wished my Pashtu was better so that I could hold a decent conversation with them. Abdul Wali returned and more food was served, after which we were presented with bundles tied in brightly patterned silk handkerchiefs. The bundles contained nuts, dried fruit and sweets;

each one was tied with a beaded tassel sewn by the women themselves. I never did discover what Abdul Wali had been doing that morning. He was rather diffident about it.

Once the celebrations were over it was time to return to Bitow. Everyone made me promise to return, and there was certainly much that needed to be done in the area. I promised to come back with some wire to try out some riverbank protection. Although I would be sorry to say goodbye to Abdul Wali and his family, who had made me feel so welcome, I would be glad to escape the fleas and regain a little privacy. I wanted to find out what had been going on in our house whilst I had been away and I wanted to see Zebedee. It had been great fun in Abqol but I would be glad to get back to what I now thought of as home.

Welcome meal in the clinic for all outreach workers.

The clinic

Nur Rajan and Khodai Mir measuring work done on Karez

The team - Sarah, Caroline, Chris and Andy.

Abdul Wadood

Abdul Garni, Abdul Hamid, Mohammed Hussein and Roz Mohammed.

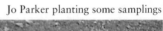

Jo Parker planting some samplings

Abdul Wahdood's Russian Jeep

Jo Parker

Buying eggs from Mular Abdul Zai

Tinsmith working outside Abdul Wahdood's House

Afgans manhandling the trestle into the stream.

Passing rocks out to (start of) bridge pier

Finished bridge (Water under the bridge)

A. Garni lighting the stove

The work room at our house

Zebedee

Chapter Five

On 1 November, the weather in our valley changed dramatically. The constant sunny skies gave way to fierce, cold winds that whipped up thick dust storms and stripped the leaves from the trees. The Afghans assured me that this was quite normal for the time of year. A few days later I had my first experience of rain since leaving England. I rushed to cover up the few remaining bags of cement that had survived our disastrous crash. Sarah had told me at the London briefing, 'you won't need cold-weather gear in Afghanistan.' Luckily, I had ignored her advice and stocked up on cold-weather gear, anticipating that, unlike Sarah's, most of my work would be out of doors. I certainly looked quite a sight in my Wellington boots, sweater and a heavy waterproof coat on top of my Afghan dress and baggy trousers.

No one would describe Afghanistan as a hospitable country. High mountains in the centre and the north are covered in snow for most of the year; when this melts in the spring, severe flooding results. The Afghan winters are extremely harsh, with temperatures dropping to -20 or –30oC in some areas while, by contrast, the summer heat in the desert can rise as high as 40 oC. Fortunately, our valley, dominated by the river, was more temperate and many of the local people were able to make a living from cultivating almonds, apricots and grapes. The fruit, when dried, was transported, together with other crops, to markets by nomadic traders. These men, with their camel trains, perform the dual role of transporter and wholesaler. Wheat and maize for local consumption were grown on irrigated fields, while rice came from the water meadows close to the river. November was the season of the rice harvest; I watched as the rice plants were laboriously cut by hand and left to dry. During the drying process, a threshing-floor was created by cutting away the undergrowth and stamping down the soil.

Despite the advent of the colder weather, we were warm enough inside the clinic, as cylindrical wood-burning stoves, called bokharis, were placed in each room. We had an early-morning ritual whereby Abdul Garni would bring us tea and light the stove in our room, fussing over it until his coaxing brought it to life. Then we would sit around the stove, wrapped in our thick cotton quilts, called brastans, munching bread and sipping tea. In this way, the room was always cosily warm by the time we were ready to get properly dressed. The health workers certainly liked warmth, so that, by the end of the day, the heat from their stove had built up to such a degree that their room was like a sauna. I found it easy, after a good supper, to doze off in the warm atmosphere, allowing the chatter of the Afghans to wash over me. At night the stoves were allowed to die down and, although we slept on mattresses on the floor, our thick quilts kept us reasonably warm. I suffered from almost permanently cold feet throughout the Afghan winter, as custom dictated that no shoes should be worn indoors and our clinic did not boast the primitive central heating that channelled hot air beneath the floors of some of the houses.

My favourite time of the day was the early morning for, although the sun rose at about 5.30, it didn't appear from behind the mountains for at least another hour. The air was still chilly at that time, but I loved the privacy. No one else was up, and I invariably found myself drawn towards the river on these solitary walks. The sound of its rushing water was always with me, even when I was indoors. As I approached it through the dawn-lit orchard, its noise became almost deafening. Standing on the gravel bank I was mesmerised, as when a child, by the magic of fast-flowing water. I felt a special connection with this river, for it was one of the main reasons for my coming to the valley. It was wonderful to think that my bridge would unite the valley's community, until now divided by this river. However, I was still uncertain of exactly how to construct a lasting bridge that would withstand the battering of the flood tides in spring. As the fast-flowing river glinted and glistened in the early-morning sunlight, I wondered how my little house by the Thames in Oxford was. I remembered my joy at finding a place so close to the river where the great love of my life, water, gurgled by day and night.

Sarah and Caroline found themselves stretched to the limit by their work in the clinic. The place was always bustling, the kitchen often full to overflowing with women waiting for attention. Earlier in the year they would have waited patiently in the orchard beside the clinic but now, as the bitter winds swept through the valley, it was far too cold for this. Caroline found herself faced with a tricky situation. The health workers she was training were all male and the husbands of the women patients refused to allow them to be examined by a man. Nor did they like the idea of their women leaving their house to visit the clinic. If this attitude was allowed to persist, once Caroline returned to England the women of the valley would receive no medical care whatsoever. She decided to enlist the help of Abdul Wahdood, the warlord, and he agreed to write to all the villagers to tell them that they must allow all women to be treated by the male health workers.

Shortly after this Caroline was surprised to receive a summons to attend one of Abdul Wahdood's stepmothers at his house. Anticipating that the woman must be very ill, she was taken aback, on her arrival, to find that it was nothing serious at all. Abdul Wahdood was forced to admit that while in principle he supported Caroline's proposal regarding the male health workers, he could not bring himself to apply it to his own family. Protecting the women of his household was a matter of honour for him. 'If I allow them to go to the clinic,' he explained, 'the next thing I know, they will be going to the bazaar. Soon they become just like you.' A terrible prospect indeed! We let the matter go, for we knew that, since he had inherited his position of power on the death of his brother, things had not been easy for him. He could not afford to do anything that would lower his status.

Caroline battled on with her attempts to change the local people's attitude to medicine. They would constantly hold out their hands, begging, 'Goli ma ta raka' ('Give me pills'). I wondered if this was partly because of the value that medicines had on the open market. Certainly local medicine men sold potions and pills for substantial amounts of money. Whilst, at one time, these men had had a knowledge of valuable herbal lore, they now dispensed a cocktail of out-of-date or banned medicines that was often lethal.

Many of the common ills in the valley could have been cured if people had known the basic rules of hygiene and diet. To try to reinforce these rules, Health Unlimited aimed to train a group of outreach workers who would travel round the villages. They would talk to the people about the simple things they could do to make a huge difference to problems like infant diarrhoea, a major cause of mortality in the very young. Recruiting suitable workers for the task was not so easy, even though the men were no longer away fighting the Communists. For a start, they needed to be able to read and write and, while Health Unlimited's school would help, literacy was still rare in the valley. The candidates had to come from families who belonged to the Harakat party, with fathers who did not need them to work on the land. We managed to recruit a dozen suitable students to attend the twelve-week course in Quetta. They gathered at the clinic, where Abdul Hadi had brewed up one of his extra-special stews as a send-off. The next morning, off they went on foot, each carrying his belongings in a little bundle at the end of a stick so that they looked like a team of Dick Whittingtons. Their bundles were so small that I wondered how they would have enough to see them through the tough journey into Pakistan, never mind the twelve weeks of the course.

I realized how overburdened with material possessions we in the West are. At first, the Afghan way of life seemed romantic to me. Despite the rigours of the climate and the discomfort of our living quarters, it had a feel of the Arabian Nights. In the evenings I would listen to the Afghans telling stories around the fire, while during the day I often caught sight of them ploughing their fields with oxen or winnowing their wheat by tossing it in the air. My romantic view was cut short when, one day in early November, a local man was shot in the leg, following some kind of dispute. It was a nasty wound and by the time he was brought to the clinic, he had lost a lot of blood. Surprisingly, Sarah had never had to deal with a gunshot wound before. When she discovered that the bone in the leg was fractured, she decided to send him to Quetta for hospitalisation. I wondered how the poor man would survive several days in the back of a pick-up truck across the bumpy roads to Quetta. My ribs, fractured in the lorry crash, were taking a long time to heal and I remembered the agony of travelling in that condition.

My romantic view of life in Afghanistan was further eroded by the conditions that women lived under. From their birth to the day they are married they live in their father's house. Marriages are usually arranged and, when a girl leaves her father, she is confined to her husband's house for the rest of her life. No careful assessment of potential partners seemed to be made by the girl's parents: it was a straightforward business transaction, with the girl being offered to whoever could pay the best bride price. Abdul Wahdood told me about a very poor man who had offered his daughter, a child barely able to walk, as a fiancée to anyone prepared to pay a price of 10,000 afghanis, enough to buy him a good poplar tree or ten sheep. I suppose you could say that, in a society like this, women are at least recognised as having a value. But Afghan parents still hope for male children. Sarah, Caroline and I were witnesses to a fascinating, but unhappy, episode that exemplified the region's attitude to marriage. Abdul Wahdood's own sister, Gulbibi, was due to be married and the three of us were invited to the ceremony. It was very different from anything I had encountered in Britain.

Gulbibi was marrying a man she had never met and, to make matters worse, he lived a long way away. For a 16-year-old girl who had never been outside her village this was a terrifying prospect. In addition, she would probably never see her mother or sisters again, as Afghan women rarely leave their homes, and never travel long distances to visit family. A wedding like this one takes place in two parts. There are celebrations for two days when the bride leaves her parents' home, and further celebrations when she arrives at her husband's house. We were invited to the bride's departure. On the first day, we arrived in the early evening and saw Gulbibi, the bride, crouched in a corner of her living-room. Her eyes were red-rimmed and I wondered whether this was because of the smoke from the fire that filled the place or whether she had been crying. Later we were shown into a room kept for special occasions. I had never seen anything like it in an Afghan house before, nor did I later. It had a beautiful wooden ceiling and under-floor central heating, and embroidered cloths decorated the walls. Gulbibi had developed a splitting headache and was again huddled in a corner. There were so many visitors coming and going and children playing everywhere that no one seemed to be paying her any attention. I couldn't think what to say to her: she looked so miserable, not at all a blushing bride full of anticipation. Most of the women went to cook, so we settled down to sleep for a while; it was obviously going to be a long night.

At about ten o'clock the dinner arrived. It was the celebratory meal we had sampled once or twice before with chicken stew, rice, yoghurt and stewed plums, and of course the inevitable boiled mutton. After dinner we were included in what, for the local women, was a very special treat. We had our hands dyed red with henna. After our palms had been smeared with it, they were bandaged up, so that we wouldn't get the dye on our clothes.

We all felt rather depressed as we walked home through the clear night air discussing Gulbibi's plight. By the time we fell exhausted into our beds, we had agreed to give the next day's celebrations a miss. But the following morning Abdul Wahdood sent someone to escort us to his house for the next part of the ceremony. It seemed impossible to refuse and, when we arrived, a large crowd had already gathered. Hordes of strange men turned out to be the groom's half of the wedding guests. When we went into the house, we had to climb over piles of trunks containing Gulbibi's luggage. As well as talking to the women of the family, we were invited to meet the groom. This was a special privilege, as we were Western women, but the young man seemed overawed by us. He looked kind and gentle, but just as scared as poor Gulbibi. As she had yet to meet him, we were able to go back to her and tell her that we liked him and thought he looked attractive and kind. She seemed unconvinced and continued to look sad and listless.

The entertainment commenced with Gulbibi's mother playing on the drum. Sarah, Caroline and I got into Julie Andrews mode with our rendition of 'Wouldn't it be Lovely?' from My Fair Lady and 'My Favourite Things' from The Sound of Music. Later, we amazed the company with a demonstration of 'The Gay Gordons' and 'The Dashing White Sergeant', modified as there were just the three of us. Then came the grand finale. Gulbibi was dressed in all her wedding finery, which she would probably have started embroidering at a very early age. She looked very beautiful in her new dress, the cuffs and bodice of which were intricately embroidered with a rainbow of beads and thread. Her trousers, also new, had beautiful embroidery on the cuffs. Her feet and hands were dyed dark red by the henna, and round her neck was a substantial necklace made of tiny glass beads, while her hair was combed and plaited with gold and silver threads. On top of this was placed a heavy headdress of beads with two long beaded pieces hanging down each side. Finally, there was a richly embroidered green shawl, swirled with gold and red flowers.

The effect was spoiled when Gulbibi, resplendent in all her finery, retired into a corner, crouched down and burst into tears, her body wracked by heart-breaking sobs. Her sister and mother joined in, and in no time at all every woman in the room was in floods of tears. We stood awkwardly, not knowing what to do, until an old woman asked us why we weren't joining in. Apparently this was quite normal in this part of the world and when we tried to explain that, in our country, people didn't usually cry at weddings, it seemed to be a concept that no one could grasp. How could a wedding be joyful, they reasoned, when such close ties were being broken?

The festivities were interrupted by an announcement from Abdul Wahdood that shooting had broken out in Gazak between rival factions and he had to go there to sort it out. Gulbibi's departure would have to be delayed until the following day, so we returned to the clinic. The next morning, to the accompaniment of the traditional rifle shots, Gulbibi set off for her new life mounted on a magnificent white horse, her wedding clothes now covered by a white burkha. Her new husband and friends walked beside her, while the trunks and boxes full of her possessions followed on two camels. Watching her ride out of sight, we wondered if she would be happy in her new life, far from the loved ones from whom she had never before been parted. One way and another, the event had been more like a wake than a wedding.

Another of Abdul Wali's sisters had a very unhappy life. She was the widow of Abdul Wahdood's elder brother, Abdullah. When her husband died, she was not allowed to return home to her family. In Afghanistan, a widow has no status and, according to custom, she was only permitted to marry one of her late husband's brothers. We were advised not to show her any kindness as, when members of the previous team had befriended her, she had been locked away for several weeks. Abdul Wahdood didn't want to marry her; for him, one wife was quite enough. In the end, she married his younger brother, Mobin. He always seemed clueless to me, but at least she was restored to the status of a married woman and escaped some of the misery that she had been subjected to.

Nevertheless, young girls were clearly dreaming of their future husbands and their heads were full of romantic ideas. One young woman I met down by the river where she was collecting water admired the cardigan I was wearing. I told her, in my best Pashtu, that my mother had made it. She told me her name was Dowlatbach and asked if I was married, so I showed her a picture of Yasser, my Egyptian boyfriend. 'Perhaps I change my name and come to England', she said. 'You might not like it', I told her. 'I will, if there are men like him there', she replied, nodding at Yasser's picture. We often met after this and I was glad of someone to talk to, as I was feeling increasingly isolated. Sarah and Caroline's close working relationship meant that they always had each other to turn to, whereas it was difficult for them to appreciate the kind of problems that I was faced with.

The local birth attendants, or wise women, were known as Dais. They were quite capable of looking after mother and baby, as long as the birth was straightforward, but Sarah was often called to attend if there was any risk of a difficult birth. When things went well, these visits were often convivial occasions and, in anticipation of this, I travelled with Sarah to a village called Mustoo, in the most northerly part of the valley controlled by Abdul Wahdood. Accompanied by Roze Mohammed, we set off along the winding mountain paths that ran beside the river. At one point we had to cross a narrow bridge, about twenty feet above the water, which consisted of nothing more than a couple of poles of poplar. I resolved that my bridge would have handrails and cross-members at the very least. We arrived at the village too late to witness the birth but saw the mother and her tiny baby, only two hours old but already tightly swaddled. On the way back we heard drums and singing and a group of women appeared dancing and waving their shawls in time to the beat of a tambour. Roze Mohammed explained that it was a wedding party and we could join in if we wished. I would have loved to, but Sarah was anxious to get back to the clinic before dark. We didn't make it, and I was grateful for a clear moonlit night as I stumbled along the stony path. There were no lights in the valley at all, and I was amazed as always at the number of stars visible in the night sky.

On another occasion, Sarah, Caroline and I started for the village of Danigilzae, with Abdul Garni as our protector. We had at least a two-hour walk ahead of us but, before we had gone very far, we met a man going in the same direction who was leading three camels. Sarah, who always had trouble with her feet, looked longingly at the animals. Noticing this, Abdul Garni spoke rapidly to the camel man, who promptly ordered his animals to kneel down. This they did very grudgingly, encouraged by a sharp thwack from the camel man's stick. Gratefully we clambered up and were shunted backwards and forwards, as the beasts of burden lurched back onto their feet. I felt like royalty, elevated above the passing countryside on my stately, if smelly, mount. We rode in style all the way to our destination; I could happily have gone on further, it felt so grand.

Despite my occasional trips with Sarah and Caroline, I still felt quite isolated. Zebedee elected to go almost everywhere with me, but I felt a little pathetic with only a cat for company. I was delighted when we received a message that two new team members would be joining us around the end of the year. Andy was a dentist and Chris a teacher. I was particularly looking forward to Chris's arrival; it would be nice to have a non-medical person around. He could be a travelling companion for me on my trips up to Gazak, as he would be working at the school there.

December arrived, and with it a deterioration in the weather. There was drizzle in the day and frost in the night. Only the thought of the two new team members arriving from England saved me from being completely depressed. I was making a detailed map of the area and it was coming on well, but I still could not get Abdul Wahdood to agree on the location of the new bridge.

Despite several meetings held in various villages, we seemed to be getting nowhere. The parties merely argued and debated. I explained how the bridge would be built, but some people said they did not want animals crossing their land and would not allow the bridge to be built there. At last I thought I had found a suitable site. I tramped around trying to measure things up and, much to the watching Afghans' amusement, squelched about with my Wellington boots full of water. What must they think of me, I wondered, wading into streams up to my knees, scarf tied round my neck, dress flapping and wellies squelching? Sadly, this site was unsuitable too, as the river there was too wide and too deep.

We were now into December and anticipating the arrival of the new team members, so it came as a shock to receive a message from Roger, the charity's field officer in Quetta, telling us to return there without delay. It was all very mysterious. We were to bring just enough for the journey, as we would be returning to Daichopan in due course. We were not to tell anyone that we were leaving. Caroline and I read the letter over and over again; we didn't know what to think. Sarah burst into a flood of tears, as she loved the valley so much and hated the journey to

Quetta. Caroline and I didn't relish the idea either, not least because our visas had expired and we would be illegal immigrants if we returned to Pakistan. Nevertheless, we started to work out what to take with us on the journey and arranged to padlock everything else into tin trunks so that it wouldn't get stolen in our absence. There was so much to organise, as we had no idea how long we would be away. We all had unfinished projects, and Sarah and Caroline were extremely worried about the welfare of their health workers and the patients under their care. To add to our misery, it began to rain non-stop. Three days later, the jeep arrived and Abdul Wahdood came to the clinic to tell us that we must leave. We were still nothing like ready to go and managed to get our departure put off for another day. Apparently there was more trouble between rival factions up at Gazak, for we found the health workers' room full of Mujahideen armed to the teeth. Caroline and Sarah dashed off to carry out a final count of the money and I drew up details of the planned latrine for the clinic in the hope that Roze Mohammed would arrange for the work to be started before I returned.

Next morning, after a quick breakfast of tea with bread, we piled everything into the jeep. I said a reluctant goodbye to Zebedee and shut him in our room, as I had a vision that, if I didn't, he'd be running after us halfway to Pakistan. It felt awful leaving him behind, but Mohammed Hussein promised to look after him. I had my doubts about this and was worried that the cat might not get enough to eat while I was away.

We set off with Abdul Wahdood and a bushy-bearded mullah, who I hadn't seen before, sitting up front beside our driver, Khodai Dahd. We three were, as usual, packed into the back, while two fierce-looking Mujahideen, who were strangers to us, sat on top of an assortment of sacks of almonds, our rucksacks, a rocket launcher and a Kalashnikov rifle. To add to the squash, Abdul Hamid got in at Tsangtmor and squeezed himself next to us so that we could hardly move. We hadn't seen him for weeks but were glad he was with us; despite his reputation as being a bit of a rogue he was also known to be exceptionally brave.

From the river we turned towards the mountains and began to climb up towards the spot where, only two months earlier, we had had our terrible accident. My heart was in my mouth long before we reached the dreaded spot. I begged Khodai Dahd to drive carefully and wondered again how anyone could think of trying to bring a heavily laden lorry up here. Thankfully our jeep was smaller and more manoeuvrable and, once we had safely passed by the place where we had left the road, I breathed comfortably again.

As we descended again and started to cross a broad plain towards the Kalat–Kandahar highway, the skies darkened and it started to rain. The jeep's engine spluttered and we ground to a halt. We had run out of petrol. Abdul Wahdood flagged down a passing motorbike and, riding pillion, he raced off in search of fuel. A short while later he returned with enough petrol to get us going again, at least as far as Macor. The town had been 'liberated' since we last passed that way and was now in the hands of the Mujahideen. Abdul Wahdood told us that we had been offered accommodation for the night in one of the traditional square mud houses there. Imagine our surprise when we were greeted by a familiar face – Gulbibi the reluctant bride. She was so pleased to see us and assured us that she was happy and well treated. We were shown into a beautiful room with glass shelves all around displaying cups and teapots. The whole room was plastered a pale creamy colour with embroidered hangings decorating the walls. Although it was cold outside, the room boasted under-floor heating which soon warmed us up. As it was only mid-afternoon and there would be a long wait for supper, I asked Abdul Wahdood if he would teach me how to say prayers. This was not so much out of religious devotion as self-preservation. I reckoned that we were less likely to be shot if I was reciting Islamic prayers. We went through the prayers slowly, as I tried to write them down phonetically. They seemed to go on for ever and I wondered how anyone could ever learn it all.

After supper, the men went to sleep in the local mosque while we lay down in the main room with Gulbibi and the other women of the house.

The under-floor heating blazed away all through the night so that, by morning, I felt like a well-done loaf of bread. At sunrise we were off again, after affectionate farewells to the smiling Gulbibi. The jeep bounced and slithered out of town for, although the rain had momentarily stopped, there was nothing but mud in every direction. In no time at all, the jeep was so plastered that it was almost impossible to see out through the windows. Joining a more substantial track, we passed a burnt-out Russian tank before we caught up with a queue of lorries stuck in the mud where the track forded a small river. Khodai Dahd revved up the engine, raced past the lorries and started up the far bank. I had to admire his sheer determination to make it to the top and his ability to hold the wildly jolting and slithering jeep on course. Somehow we made it but, before we had gone very far, our way was barred by another queue of lorries. A vehicle had skidded half off the road with its front wheels in the ditch. There was no way round, so we decided to head back the way we had come. Turning off the main track, we attempted a detour. The jeep was jumping around like a bucking bronco, but we were making some progress. As we drove over one particularly large pot-hole there was a loud crack and my seat shot forward. The main strut which supported the front of it had broken so that I was now subjected to a violent back-and-forth motion, as well as the up-and-down one we had already been suffering.

The periodic prayer stops were very welcome, as they gave my poor body a chance to recover from the acute discomfort of riding on the broken seat.

At last the skies cleared and, as the weather brightened up, so did our spirits. Khodai Dahd gave us his rendition of the latest Afghan pop songs and we responded with our version of the Beatles' 'Yellow Submarine'. Prayer stops were also pee stops for us girls and, as we trotted off behind the nearest building to relieve ourselves, we prayed that we wouldn't step on a land mine.

The last leg of the journey to the border with Pakistan was a nightmare. The rain came through the canvas roof of the jeep and before long we were soaked through. I was constantly thrown this way and that on the broken seat and my injured ribs, still not completely healed from the crash three months previously, were in agony. We drove long into the night; how Khodai Dahd could see the road ahead was beyond me. So much mud was thrown up onto the glass of the headlamps that their light was almost obscured. At last, our jeep reached the border town of Badini and we wound our way past rows of deserted lorries until we reached the Harakat party HQ. Once inside, Abdul Wahdood lit the fire that served the under-floor heating system. It was too dark to make out our surroundings. All ten of us lay down on the warm floor crammed in like a tin of sardines.

It wasn't until the next morning that we were able to see the room properly. It had a rush-matting ceiling and pictures of alpine scenes on the walls. The Afghans brewed tea and Abdul Hamid produced some bread, nuts and dried apricots for us. We set off at about nine and I was surprised to see, after the relatively deserted Afghan roads, a long queue of traffic winding its way at a snail's pace along the dirt road. We were now back in Pakistan, and every time Khodai Dahd risked life and limb to career past a particularly slow-moving lorry in the queue, Caroline and I pulled our burkhas over our faces, as our visas had expired. Sarah was all right for, on a previous trip, she had secured an indefinite visa through an official sympathetic to Health Unlimited. There was no stopping for prayers now. On and on we went, higher and higher into the brown mountains, brown like heaps of demerara sugar. There were very few people about, just a shepherd with a flock of thin, ragged sheep. A sprinkling of snow on the brown mountains lay like icing sugar on the demerara. The road wound ever upwards until we reached the summit and had a breathtaking view of multi-coloured mountains stretching endlessly out before us. The extraordinary light turned them green, red, blue and pink as we began our descent and, by the time we reached the main road at the foot of the mountains, the day was over and darkness had overtaken us once more.

That night we stayed in a small town. I was so tired that I hardly noticed the house or the room. I just remember that I fell straight asleep. It seemed only a few minutes later that a flood of bright light invaded my dreams. In fact it was morning and we were back in the land of the electric light bulb. We staggered out to a disgusting latrine and had a quick wash under an outside tap. Caroline was asked to look at our host's father, a man of seventy with a wife forty years his junior. He appeared to have little or nothing wrong with him but demanded to be given pills, at which Caroline muttered under her breath that she was tired of dealing with hypochondriacs.

Now that we were in Pakistan, we could no longer use the jeep, as it had Afghan registration plates. Another vehicle was found, but that was only able to take us as far as the outskirts of Quetta. There, for some reason, we had to transfer to yet another car and we were left squatting on the ground in our burkhas, ignored by all, while the Afghans went in search for a suitable vehicle. By the time we reached Dr Haquani's guest house it was almost dusk. Roger Doran, from Health Unlimited, was there to meet us and, of course, the first thing we did was to demand, 'Why on earth did you call us back from Afghanistan?' 'Because', he answered, 'the money's run out, and Jo here – he turned to me, 'is wanted by Military Intelligence!'

Chapter Six

There was no money? I was a spy? My mind was racing. I had stepped into some crazy nightmare. Everyone in the room was stunned by Roger's announcement but, within seconds, we'd recovered enough to start deluging him with questions. Gradually, the mystery unfolded. The ODA was supposed to fund our stay in Afghanistan and the work of the clinic. However, this was dependent upon Health Unlimited matching their contribution with money from other donors. The World Health Organisation (WHO) was to have produced the other half but, with the continuing fighting in Afghanistan and renewed threats to Westerners, donor countries were getting cold feet and WHO had withdrawn. As several aid workers and others from the West had recently been kidnapped or killed, this was not surprising but it did mean that what I'd come out to achieve was now in jeopardy. The proposals that I had submitted for a bridge, a tree nursery and irrigation improvements had not been accepted. Sarah and I were going to have to talk to the agencies and convince them to give us the money.

The mystery surrounding Military Intelligence and their interest in me had a simple and ironic explanation. Roger had received a telephone call from a stern Pakistani gentleman claiming to be the head of the Pakistani Military Intelligence. He wanted to know where I was. Roger, sensing trouble, was vague in his reply. He then called the British Consulate, who confirmed that Brigadier Wahid Mohammed was indeed the head of the Pakistani Military Intelligence. As soon as I heard the name, I laughed, much to Roger's surprise and annoyance. 'Don't you realise the seriousness of the situation you're in?' he asked. 'Relax, Roger, there's a very simple explanation for all this. My mother and I were out here on holiday a few years back and, on our travels, we met up with a charming gentleman who said he was a retired army officer. His name was Brigadier Wahid Mohammed. I guess he's not retired after all – he's Pakistan's answer to MI5.' I knew that my mother had corresponded with the brigadier after our return to England and I assumed that she must have, rather unwisely, told him I was in Pakistan. I just hoped she hadn't said I was en route to Afghanistan.

I faxed my mother, asking her to write to the brigadier to tell him that I was sorry to have missed him but had decided to go on to India. Hopefully this would defuse a tricky situation, but I would still have to lie low, as my visa for Pakistan was out of date. Sarah and Caroline were furious at being dragged away from their work in the Daichopan clinic and they made it clear that they blamed me for much of this. Although I apologised to them, they refused to speak to me and went to bed without speaking, leaving me feeling desolate and alone. I couldn't go to bed, as I had been ostracised by my roommates. Thinking I had jeopardised the whole project, I burst into tears.

The next morning Roger was up early and found me in the armchair in the sitting-room. He didn't seem to notice that my eyes were red and swollen from crying but, when he asked where everyone had slept, I told him that the other two women were in the bedroom and I had spent the night in the armchair. He was mystified, so I explained that it appeared that I was a security risk and was endangering the whole project. Roger was very sympathetic and told me that it was the two new team members, Chris and Andy, whom he considered a security risk, not me. This was why he had sent them to Swat, a scenic area in northern Pakistan. He had encouraged them to take a holiday, as he considered them something of a liability in Quetta. Roger explained that Andy, the dentist, was even more inexperienced at aid work than I was. His only experience of life outside Europe had been a holiday in Turkey – hardly suitable training for life in a remote part of Afghanistan. But the real problem was Chris. Whilst Andy was a quiet soul, Chris, the teacher, never stopped talking. He had had considerable experience abroad and exuded confidence – too much of it for Roger's liking. Also, both men seemed to have no idea how to deal with Asians. Andy just couldn't understand them, while Chris thought they were 'a load of ignorant peasants'. I wasn't quite as excited about having two new members on the team as I had been. It was several days later that I met the pair of them and the meeting was anything but happy. I was on my own, working on one of my proposals, when the two men came. 'So, you're the one who's caused all the trouble then', said the bigger of the two. He was certainly not the most attractive man I'd ever seen – well over six foot tall, broad-shouldered, with a bald head and no eyelashes or eyebrows. My answer was not a very polite one but Andy, the dentist, quickly stepped in to offer a more welcoming greeting. He looked extremely young, with dark wavy hair, quite a contrast to his hulking, hairless companion. Nothing that happened subsequently changed my first impression of Chris. I had always taken care not to do anything that might undermine Sarah's authority. Chris had no such scruples. He made it clear from the outset that he was not impressed with either Roger's or Sarah's administrative abilities and proceeded to take over as many aspects of the project as he could. He never seemed to be happy with anyone's decisions – except his own.

Abdul Wahdood had prepared some outline costs which he wrote laboriously in his curly Arabic script, using the alternative numbering system prevalent in central Asia. Chris queried all the figures, voicing his doubts about their ability to handle money. After one such meeting Abdul Wahdood called in to see me. 'Many battles I have seen.' He sighed. 'Now I have another one with this teacher.' It seemed so unfair that this great man of action should be burdened with fighting a bully like Chris over school accounts.

I have to admit that Chris's knowledge of various aspects of life in Pakistan was quite extensive. He had read a great deal about Islam and spoke warmly about many aspects of the religion. However, he didn't seem to carry this warmth over to the people who practised the religion and was scathing about both Pakistanis and Afghans. I was concerned that this could severely damage our team's relationship with the local Afghans. However, Abdul Wahdood was very restrained with the uncouth giant, patiently going over and over the figures with him without complaint.

Chris was constantly reminding us of his extensive overseas experience and his prowess as a sportsman, only hampered by a serious car accident, which he claimed had prevented him from becoming a professional footballer. As he felt he should be in charge of everything all the time, and I had no intention of letting him tell me how to run the technical side of things, our relationship didn't improve. I was able to keep my distance from Chris most of the time as, when he and Andy returned from their trip north, the small guest house where we were staying was unable to accommodate all of us. Sarah, Caroline and I moved back to Joelle's house, where we had previously stayed when in Quetta. It was winter and quite as cold as England at this time of year, with a bitter wind swirling down the streets where the dust of summer had turned to the mud of winter. Everywhere in these muddy streets people huddled around small kerosene fires to keep warm, and the air was thick with smoke from open fires and chimneys.

I was kept busy rewriting the proposals for my work in order to raise some cash, and was lucky to have help in this from a man called Wayne Bauman, who was running the UNDP (United Nations Development Programme) office in Quetta. He kindly went through my proposals with me, explaining where there had been queries and what amendments I could make to satisfy these. He was very supportive and keen to see my irrigation project and the bridge-building get underway. However, the office of the UNDP in Peshawar, which had to approve all funding applications, didn't like my bridge. They thought that my simple structure, using wire gabions filled with rocks plus local poplar poles, was far too small-time for them to consider. They favoured a bigger bridge altogether, made of metal parts bolted together on the site, rather like the ones used by the British army. The project seemed to be growing and growing and I was concerned that it was getting out of hand. In the end they turned me down, but luckily I could use some of the funds which Oxfam had let me have earlier. If we were careful, we could fund the cost of the poplar beams this way and we'd already purchased some wire for trials of work to protect the river bank. Maybe this could be used to make the gabions to hold the rocks. I did better with my irrigation project, but the main issues still to be settled were: how to get the money into Afghanistan, how to audit the payment of wages, and how to measure achievement. Abdul Wahdood and I devised a simple system. Payment would be on a piecework system – the workers would only be paid for the work they did. As most of them couldn't write their name, they would acknowledge receipt of their wages by their thumbprint.

The overall achievement of the scheme would be measured by assessing the flow of water before and after the renovation. I had to work out how to do this, so I came up with a sort of 'Pooh-sticks' idea. All I had to do was drop a twig into the water and see how long it took to go a metre. My father managed to send me a sailor's digital compass, which incorporated a stopwatch. This instrument was designed for use in sailing races but it came in very handy for measuring the water flow. Unknowingly, my father had provided me with the means to measure the progress of my 'Pooh-sticks'.

I rewrote the proposals for submission to the UNDP in Peshawar to meet their guidelines, but their approval was not expected until the New Year. There was no way we could hang around in Quetta for that long and anyway, I was a wanted woman and I needed to get out quickly; I had no idea what the brigadier might do if he discovered my whereabouts. I might well get packed onto the next plane back to the UK. The last thing I wanted was to be deprived of a return to the valley I'd grown to love so much and not to be able to complete my important work there.

The other vital project I wanted to see under way was the planting of fruit trees, so vital to the livelihood of the valley people. I was refused funding for this, as I was not qualified in either forestry or agriculture.

I was extremely disappointed at this until one of the staff with FAO (the Food and Agriculture Organisation) mentioned that they were growing fruit tree saplings at Swat in preparation for taking them into Afghanistan. I could apply for some of these but there would be a delay in agreeing the funding. The same old Catch-22 – I couldn't afford to wait and the money couldn't be hurried. I discussed the problem with Abdul Wahdood, who suggested Abdul Hamid should stay behind and wait for the money and the fruit-tree saplings, then accompany them into Afghanistan.

Knowing Abdul Hamid's reputation, I was a little dubious of this idea. However, I figured that we must be able to make the man fully accountable for the money and the trees: I knew exactly what we should be receiving. Abdul Wahdood promised to make clear to Abdul Hamid how important it was that both trees and money arrived safely. I felt he was secretly relieved that whatever problems or disagreements had occurred between him and Abdul Hamid could be overcome by this arrangement. It restored Abdul Hamid's status since he could justifiably claim to be treated as an honoured and trusted member of the project team. When I took Abdul Hamid to the UNDP and FAO offices to finalise arrangements, I noticed that his suave and sophisticated façade crumbled away and he appeared, for once, to be unsure of himself. He obviously realised the responsibility of the task he had been given – transporting what to an Afghan was an immense sum of money. As he struggled to make arrangements with UN officials and other expats, I saw his English strained to the limits. Eventually everything was arranged, including a bank account for Health Unlimited, although they had no official status in Pakistan. I breathed a sigh of relief that some of my worries had been taken care of, but then a phone call from England threw us into turmoil again. Caroline's father had been taken seriously ill with a viral infection of the brain. Obviously Caroline had to fly home immediately, but nothing in Pakistan is easy. First of all she had to get an exit visa as, like mine, her visitor's visa had run out. The British Consulate was very helpful, and while they were sorting out the visa, we set about getting her a seat on a plane to the UK. We had to ring the airport, and the only place we could call to destinations outside Quetta was Dr Haqani's guest house, where we had been staying until the arrival of Chris and Andy. After frantically calling all the airlines and agents, we were told that she could have a ticket if she collected it right away. Paul, an aid worker who was also staying at Joelle's, offered to chauffeur her in his Land Cruiser. Off they raced to get the ticket and, by some miracle, thirty-six hours after learning about her father's condition, Caroline was on her way to London, complete with ticket and exit visa. She promised that, if her father's condition improved, she would return to us as soon as possible. As Abdul Hamid was having to hang around for several weeks to take delivery of the trees and the money, it was agreed that, should she return during that time, he would accompany Caroline back into Afghanistan. I had almost forgotten that the next day was Christmas Eve when Abdul Wahdood announced that was when we should leave Pakistan, as the weather looked likely to be fair for some days to come. That evening we treated ourselves to a slap-up meal at the smart Serena Hotel. After all, we were going back into the wildest part of Afghanistan where even the word 'primitive' couldn't do justice to the local cuisine.

On Christmas Eve I rose early and took the last shower I was likely to enjoy for some time. We assembled at the guest house, where Chris and Andy had their first taste of what it is like to be a woman in a Muslim country. As neither of them had beards, and they certainly didn't have a word of Pashtu, they were going to have to make the journey dressed as women. Chris's huge bulk inside a burkha stretched the credibility of his disguise to the limit. He didn't take kindly to the idea of taking on the persona of a Muslim woman, even for a short while, and I thought it served him right for his condescending remarks about Afghans. Once we were in our finery, a pick-up truck arrived to collect us. As usual, in true Afghan style, it was a tremendous squash. Although we had lost Caroline and Abdul Hamid, we now acquired an Afghan woman, the sister of one of our bodyguards. She was coming along for the ride and to lend an air of authenticity. We also had Chris and Andy, plus all their luggage, which included an inflatable canoe and a mountain of personal effects that Chris had brought. I bristled at the thought of my problems at Heathrow airport on the way out, but at least the boys had brought the tripod for my surveying-level out with them. I was delighted to be reunited with it.

At the town of Muslimabad, about an hour's drive from Quetta, we stopped at a wayside garage, had lunch and transferred to the jeep. As we piled back in, I discovered that the seat that had broken on our original journey had not been mended. My ribs ached at the thought of it, so Abdul Wahdood decided to take the jeep off and seek a repair. He couldn't risk letting us and all the luggage be seen so, together with one of the bodyguards and the Afghan woman, we were left by the roadside surrounded by piles of trunks and sacks.

Time went by. One hour and then two. Where was our warlord? We huddled together for warmth and munched a few biscuits. We began to wonder if the jeep had been stopped by the police. Suppose Abdul Wahdood didn't come back? What would we do? At last the jeep returned, but it stopped at some distance from us. Abdul Wahdood climbed down and approached us. Our fears had been well founded. The police had been tipped off that the jeep had foreigners in it and they wanted a bribe of 500 rupees to let us proceed. As it was only about £15 we agreed; none of us wanted the whole project to be jeopardised by this one payment.

We spent the first night at the house we had stayed in on our previous journey. Sarah and I had to sleep in the main part, which was full of other guests, so early the next morning we were wakened by the sound of babies crying and women chattering. No chance of a lie-in, even on Christmas Day! We had an early lunch, which you could term Christmas dinner, except that it was just potato stew. However, we had bought some Christmas cake in a little French bakery in Quetta and that went down very well.

We set off again at about midday, still in our burkhas and covering our faces whenever we passed through a village. As we travelled on, my feet got colder and colder. When the Afghans stopped for their afternoon prayers Sarah, Andy and I knelt on our coats and said our own prayers for Christmas Day. It was well after dark when we stopped for the night and were hustled into a vast building at the back of a lodging house. I realised as I looked around that we were to spend Christmas night in a barn – strangely fitting, I thought with wry amusement. I had just drifted off to sleep when I was awakened by Abdul Wahdood. When I looked at my watch I saw it was only half past three and asked him what was going on. He told me that we needed to make an early start and began to herd us outside. I didn't believe him; it seemed more likely that there was some kind of security problem, but I never found out the truth.

Off we went in the jeep while it was still pitch-dark. Just as it was beginning to get light, we drove through a huge icy puddle and got stuck. Khodai Dahd's driving skills couldn't shift us and we had to climb down and dig the vehicle out with our bare hands. I made a mental note to warn future teams to insist on a spade being included for all trips into Afghanistan. We got the jeep free from the puddle, but then Abdul Wahdood announced that we had been driving in the wrong direction and were lost. We kept going until we came to a village where Abdul Wali went to ask for directions. He returned with a bunch of young men and they all squeezed in beside the driver. We now had five people in the front seat and so, jammed in like sardines, we drove on to the next village where we stopped for fuel. A little further on we passed a tank slowly winding its way along the track with Afghans clinging all over it and sitting on its long gun-barrel. At last we reached our overnight stop at the village of Gilan. How different it was from the 'no room at the inn' scenario of the previous night. We were ushered into a delightful hotel and taken to an upstairs room hung with fabric. A wonderful warmth rose from the under-floor heating and I wished we could have stayed there every night.

We were almost back in our valley, and as we wound our way up through the hills I pointed out to Chris and Andy the point where we had crashed off the road on our first journey into Afghanistan. I was delighted to notice that the talkative Chris fell silent for several minutes at the thought of our near-fatal accident. Perhaps he was all talk? Perhaps inside that huge body was a frightened little schoolboy? I couldn't make up my mind about him. He'd certainly not endeared himself to me. As for his silly raft! According to him, he was an expert white-water rafter and, having heard there was a river near the clinic, he was anticipating being able to show off his skills with a paddle!

We reached our valley and I was just happy to be back. Chris expressed great frustration at not being able to start straight away for Gazak and the school there. Andy was suffering from culture shock. Apart from the lack of privacy, everything was much dirtier and far more primitive than he'd imagined. Sarah wasn't happy at getting bogged down in accounts almost from the moment she got out of the jeep. Zebedee gave me the cold shoulder on my return, which is not unusual behaviour for a cat whose owner has upped and left him unexpectedly. He soon forgave me, as my bed was a warm place to sleep.

Our house and the clinic extension were far from finished, so everywhere was bursting at the seams. Sarah and I were back in our original room, but this time we had to fit in the stores for our new house as well as Chris and Andy's luggage. The room looked like a cross between a scrap-metal merchants and a stationery warehouse. Chris and Andy slept in the clinic consulting-room which meant that they had even less privacy than we did. To make matters worse, Abdul Wahdood insisted on holding his meetings at the clinic as he said that it was 'everybody's place'. He said that his house would not be seen as 'neutral territory', while the local party headquarters, the Jebha, was little more than a donkey-shed with a tent attached. He didn't seem inclined to tell us what the meetings were about but I guessed they were a gathering together of representatives from various other parties. On top of all this, the outreach workers who had gone to Quetta for training arrived back at this point and had to be accommodated in the clinic until they returned to their home. In the midst of all this chaos, I mislaid the keys to my trunk. Although I had a spare pair, I was worried that, if any of the Afghans found them, they might not give them back without first taking a look in my trunk and helping themselves to anything they fancied.

Despite the crush, we unpacked our Christmas decorations and put them up around the clinic. Having been deprived of a proper Christmas on our journey back from Quetta, we were determined to celebrate the festive season, even if we were somewhat after the event. As Andy's birthday fell on 29 December, Sarah and I tried to make it a special event, to help him feel more at home. We had brought a fruit cake back with us from Quetta, and I used a pestle and mortar to grind up some sugar until it was so fine it could pass for icing sugar. We even found three candles to stick into the cake. Abdul Hadi bought a chicken and made a delicious stew for the occasion, a welcome relief from boiled mutton. At the appointed moment he appeared through the kitchen hatch with the cake in his hands, complete with lighted candles. The Afghans found all this hugely entertaining, although they never celebrated birthdays themselves. No sooner had we celebrated Andy's birthday than it was our New Year and an excuse for yet more celebrations. It was more like Christmas than New Year, as we had some traditional English stuffing to go with a chicken plus real Christmas pudding and custard. The Afghans weren't at all sure about stuffing or Christmas pudding but they loved the custard.

After the meal, we played tapes of Chrismas carols and sang along with them. The Afghans' contribution to the celebrations was a demonstration of some of their traditional games. These appeared wildly funny to them but we were nonplussed by the whole thing. Before I went to Quetta I had written out the words of the hokey cokey, as a way of helping the Afghans' English and, on request, they performed it magnificently, singing over and over, "You put your left foot in, your left foot out, your left foot in and shake it all about ... " At this point Abdul Wahdood arrived with a couple of Mujahideen and watched while Sarah and I showed everyone how to rock 'n' roll and Mohammed Hussein demonstrated some Afghan dancing. Abdul Wahdood left quietly just before midnight and I remarked to Roze Mohammed that it was a shame he would miss 'Auld Lang Syne'. Roze Mohammed whispered that this was why he had left. He knew that 'Auld Lang Syne' involved men and women joining hands and this was not something the warrior would want his fighters to witness. As midnight approached, I did an impression of Big Ben, with my arms sticking stiffly together in the air, fingers pointing upwards. At the appointed hour, I let out twelve bongs in what I hoped was a fair approximation of Big Ben. When our New Year chased out the old, we did indeed join hands and sing 'Auld Lang Syne'. It was the first time I had spent Christmas and New Year away from home, and yet I didn't feel the slightest bit homesick.

The new year did not begin well. The next morning, when Abdul Garni brought us our tea and bread, he also brought the keys to my trunk, which he had found outside our room. I had my suspicions, the more so when I found that my precious Swiss-army knife had disappeared. Losing it was a blow as, with the kind of work I was undertaking, I was finding it invaluable. I felt sure that Abdul Garni had taken it. I had no way of proving it, but I wanted it back. I had a brainwave and announced that, if anyone found my penknife, they could have it after we left. Surprise, surprise, Abdul Garni produced it and I agreed that he should keep it after my departure. Of course he realised that I, and everyone else, knew perfectly well what had happened, but honour had been preserved.

With the new year, Mullah Ahmed Zai, the uncle with the gammy leg, joined Khodai Mir as an assistant to me but, as I feared, he was more of a hindrance than a help. Still, at least I could visit other areas of the valley more easily. I was careful to agree exactly what duties each would be expected to perform. Mullah Ahmed Zai would accompany me to the villages where I was going to complete a questionnaire to find out how much land had been destroyed, how many people lived in each village, and whether these villages had a well. Khodai Mir was going to walk up and down the valley with me, while I collected various pieces of information to extend my map of the area.

The first village I visited with Mullah Ahmed Zai, Alu, wasn't too far from the clinic. This was where Abdul Wahdood's late brother, Abdullah, had apparently killed the local Amir and taken his title. His triumph was short-lived. He died from a cancer brought on by excessive use of drugs – drugs he insisted on taking in the hope of making more male children. Having only recently discovered this piece of rather barbaric local history, I approached this particular village with some trepidation. We went first to an impressive house in the centre of the village that had fortress-like turrets at each corner. On entering through a huge wooden door, we crossed an entrance hall to be faced with another large door. This in turn opened onto a vast courtyard with five enormous mulberry trees growing in the centre. Mullah Ahmed Zai led me to a room off the courtyard where three men sat. A young lad joined us accompanied by two women. One of them was young but the other was old and wizened with age. I had carefully rehearsed my questions in Pashtu, but the Mullah was no help at all in translating the answers I received. I had to ask people to repeat their answers over and over again until I had got the gist.

I wondered who owned this grand house, which had once belonged to the dead Amir, but I didn't like to ask. Before long, we were joined by a group of farmers who worked on the estate that went with this fine house. They were wet with snow from working in the severe winter conditions. Realising that a good meal would prepare me for going out and braving the elements again, I readily agreed when we were invited to stay for lunch. I wasn't at all sure I'd made the right decision when the meal arrived. It turned out to be a disgusting version of scrambled egg, swimming in grease! After the meal we took our leave, but we hadn't walked more than a few yards through the falling snow when the young man we'd seen at lunch rushed after us and offered us a much needed umbrella. Obviously I wasn't going to get much mapping done until the weather changed. That night I was woken up by Sarah trying to reposition her mattress as melting snow was coming through the roof and dripping on her. I helped her as best I could in the limited space.

Early in the morning, I went outside to discover that it had stopped snowing and that there was a sight that quite took my breath away. I had always loved seeing the sun come up over the mountains but now everything was covered with a thick carpet of snow that gleamed pink and gold in the sunrise. Zebedee followed me out of the clinic; it was obvious that he couldn't believe his eyes. He'd never seen snow before and, as he sank into it up to his tummy, he started to progress through it with little kangaroo-like leaps. He looked more than ever like Zebedee, his bouncing namesake. He shot up a tree, showering me with powdered snow and then jumped down and disappeared completely in the stuff. After that there was no stopping him; he tore around, chasing imaginary enemies and burying himself deep in the snow.

As the snow had stopped, I grabbed the opportunity to visit another of the villages on my list. It proved a hazardous affair since we had to cross the river by the footbridge made of poplar trunks which, still coated in snow, was extremely slippery. I was surprised how well Mullah Ahmed Zai managed, considering his crippled leg, ancient shoes and lack of socks. I was appalled to see his feet clad in this way with temperatures near freezing, and offered him a pair of my own socks. Later in the day I returned and collected Khodai Mir, and we set off to do some mapping of the area. He wasn't much of an assistant; even over the roughest terrain, he never offered a hand to guide me and he was loath to carry anything for me. Thus I was saddled with all the paraphernalia that I needed for the job – cameras, notebook and a compass. Most of it could hang round my neck and I must have looked a fine sight dressed in a large baggy dress, shawl, trousers, wellies, my waterproof jacket and with all sorts of objects dangling round my neck.

I found Khodai Mir infuriating. He was always looking for an excuse not to work and a couple of times cried off sick with unconvincing ailments. As the days passed, I developed a routine of going out in the morning with Mullah Ahmed Zai to visit one of the villages and then, after lunch, trudging off with my reluctant assistant, Khodai Mir, to carry on mapping the valley. My understanding had been that one of Chris's jobs would be to teach English to the health workers. He was supposed to do the same for my assistants. When he refused to do this, I had to set to and teach them myself. Mullah Ahmed Zai made little or no progress and every day I had to go back to the beginning, as he appeared to have forgotten everything I'd taught him. Thankfully, Khodai Mir proved to be a very quick learner and was soon stringing sentences together.

The business of the English lessons was just one of the many problems with Chris that began to emerge. He was one of those people who delight in poking their nose into other people's business, while omitting to do their own tasks. He would lecture me on what was needed for the valley in the way of roads and tell Sarah what supplies she should buy and how she should manage the project. The Afghans didn't know what to make of him. On one hand they admired him because he behaved like a big, loud, overgrown schoolboy and so did they. He had studied aikido for years and was only too ready to take one of them on in a fight. But they realised that he did not trust them and they hated that. This came out quite early on in his stay in Daichopan when the Afghans objected to him wandering off on his own around the area. Chris jumped to the conclusion that they wanted to control him. The truth was that our team was under the protection of Abdul Wahdood and, if anything had befallen one of us, it would have spelt dishonour for the warlord. Something else that drove a wedge between Chris and the local people was his miner's light. He had a little lamp on a strap that went around the head. This was extremely useful in a location like ours that was without any proper lighting both inside and outside of the clinic. He was devoted to this lamp; it was certainly a lot more use to him than his inflatable raft. As Chris and Andy had to sleep in the consulting room because of the lack of space for us all in the clinic, they often left personal possessions there during the day. Not a good idea! Chris's miner's light went missing. I think the Afghans saw it there, had a good look at it and, like kids, decided to play a joke on him and hide it. Not a good idea either! He went crazy and, from that day on, he never showed any of them an ounce of trust or respect. It was not a happy situation and it was to get very much worse. We weren't to know it, but Chris would eventually jeopardise all our efforts.

Chapter Seven

N one of us could wait for the school at Gazak to be finished, so that Chris could go up there to teach and we would be rid of him. Just as this was about to happen, a tragedy occurred. Abdul Wahdood's father, the most important and powerful person in the area, died.

Early one morning, one of Akenzader's servants banged on the clinic door. When we opened up, he told us that the old man was seriously ill. Sarah, who was barely awake, wasn't sure whether she should go or not, as the 89-year-old, who always seemed as strong as an ox, was constantly calling for pills and potions, particularly ones that would make him more virile. Sarah told the servant to go away and that she'd come along later when she'd woken up properly. A short time later, the man was back again, wailing hysterically. It was almost impossible to make out what he was saying, but we managed to calm him down enough to understand – Akenzader was dead.

Sarah and I hurried to Abdul Wahdood's house and found him and the women of the family huddled together in the corner of one of the rooms, crying quietly. When I took their hands in mine to say hello the women clung to me, which surprised me. Until that moment I had not found Afghans to be very tactile but now, when I put my arm around one of Abdul Wahdood's sisters, she turned and sobbed into my chest. This was a different kind of grief to that displayed at Gulbibi's wedding where, although the young bride and her mother were clearly very upset, the other women seemed to be joining in as if it were part of a ritual. Here, the old man's family appeared stunned that the revered head of their household, the patriarch, was gone.

The women led me into the room where Akenzader had died. There he was – lying in the corner as if asleep. He'd had a good innings, I thought, but I found that I was crying too. Not for the old man, who'd moved on to another place, but for Abdul Wahdood and those who were left behind. One of the women crossed to the body and pulled back the blanket that had been covering him. The sight of the dead man moved me far less than the plight of his family. He lay there, a pale old man, looking like a waxwork. No longer the lively head of household, directing the comings and goings of twenty-five people or more. He had been a man who superintended the running of a farm of many acres, someone who grabbed your hand whenever he saw you and demanded, 'Where are my pills?' Abdul Wahdood, Ahmed Zai and some of the other mullahs came in and measured the body. They produced a piece of white cloth and tore it up; the women started to sew it. They were making his shroud. As everyone was so intent upon what they were doing and no longer seemed to notice me, I quietly left the house. A man on the roof of Abdul Wahdood's house was shouting loudly, while from the village and across the river I could hear fainter shouts. This was how they passed important news across the country. With a system like that, who needs telephones?

I wondered how Abdul Wahdood would manage, now that he had become the head of a household of twenty-three women and children and with only his 15-year-old brother to share the load. I had noticed that the young warlord seemed unable to cope with Afghan women. He hardly ever spoke to either his wife or his mother. Running a farm didn't seem like something he would be much good at either. What he was good at was politics, negotiation and diplomacy. In Britain he would probably have made it to a post in the cabinet. Abdul Wahdood was a man who preferred to talk rather than fight, something very rare in Afghanistan. He once said to me, 'If I kill a man, his family will only come and kill me, so what's the point?' It wouldn't be long before this young man's political skill would be tested to the limit.

I reckoned that Abdul Wahdood was short of money, as his sister

Gulbibi's wedding must have cost a fortune. Now he would have to foot the bill for a grand funeral for Akenzader. Under Islamic law, this had to be held as soon as possible after death. This was a very sensible rule, considering how hot it is in most Islamic countries. Preparations began almost at once, as many people were expected for the event, Akenzader having been by far the most important person in the region. One of the most important tasks was to strengthen the existing bridge across the river. I had yet to start on my new, hopefully stronger, one, so off we went, a band of volunteers and myself, armed with hammers and nails, to shore up the existing structure. After we'd done the best we could, I walked back to the clinic, past the site of our new, and still incomplete, house. Huge iron cauldrons and piles of firewood lay in the courtyard and this was obviously where the funeral feast would take place.

When I met Abdul Wahdood, I thought he had aged ten years since his father died. I was terribly disappointed when he asked our team not to attend the funeral. I would have loved to witness such a unique event and would probably never get the chance again during my stay in Afghanistan. A number of important people from outside the area were expected for the funeral and it was felt that they might be offended by the presence of foreigners. Reluctantly, we all agreed, except Chris, always a law unto himself, who decided that he wanted to see exactly what went on. So, come the day, he climbed to the top of a nearby hill, where he could get a grandstand view of the ceremony without being observed. He told us that that there must have been at least two thousand people at the funeral. Although I couldn't be present at the event, I did peep round the edge of the clinic as the crowd streamed by on their way there. I'm sure Chris was right; it seemed like an endless stream – hundreds and hundreds of people filing past, interspersed with riders on horses, with their decorated bridles and colourful saddlecloths.

When it was over, Mohammed Hussein returned to the clinic and we walked to the graveyard, high up on a hill overlooking the valley. As we gazed at the newly turned earth on Akenzader's grave, Mohammed Hussein told us that a school was to be built there in his memory.

I reflected how quiet it was and how peaceful – a perfect resting-place for a great man.

We walked back down the hill into the valley and my thoughts turned to Abdul Wahdood. With his all-powerful father dead, his position in the area was no longer secure and a power struggle could well ensue. If our protector were to lose this, our position, and the whole of the aid work in the area, could be in jeopardy. Abdul Wahdood's cousin, Mohammed Zai, would be likely to make a bid for power. His father, Kaka Jann, the late Akenzader's brother, would obviously support his son who, because of his immense size and equally large appetite, was known as 'hundred-ton man'. These two, Mohammed Zai and his father, had been the main objectors to the proposed site of my new bridge. They were a rather unpleasant couple and members of the militant Hisb'e Islam party, so things could turn very nasty for us. Another contender was Abdul Hamid, currently waiting in Quetta for Caroline and our money. He was Abdul Wahdood's number two and had great respect for him but this was no guarantee that he would not oppose him. We reckoned that news of Akenzader's death was bound to reach him pretty swiftly and Sarah remarked that perhaps he would hold Caroline hostage to force Abdul Wahdood to relinquish power. Although we thought this far-fetched, we agreed, just to be on the safe side, to be packed and ready to leave at a moment's notice.

The next day the situation had changed greatly, and not in our favour. Abdul Wahdood told us that he had handed in his resignation to the party and asked them to find someone else to be commander, as he was now overburdened with family responsibilities. Chris called it a pre-emptive move and said that, as a political tactic, it made a lot of sense. Resigning was a drastic thing to do. Either it would force a vote of confidence in the warlord and ensure his position, or he would be enabled to bow out gracefully. It may have been an astute move but it made us extremely nervous. There was nothing we could do, except sit tight with our bags packed. Abdul Wahdood had asked that a new leader be chosen within the next ten days. We got very tense during this waiting period and I snapped at Sarah, which I instantly regretted. She was not in a good mood herself. Not only was she a team leader who had no idea what was going to happen to her team, but she was concerned about her close friend Roze Mohammed, who had gone to the bazaar some days previously to buy supplies. She was worried that he would not know about the death of Akenzader, of whom he was extremely fond. Two days after the funeral, a string of camels arrived laden with supplies. The hustle and bustle of unloading the camels, checking the goods and trying to find somewhere to put everything in the clinic served temporarily to take our minds off the political scene. I didn't see Roze Mohammed arrive back from his trip to the bazaar in the jeep. When I walked into the clinic some time later and found him there, I didn't recognise him at first, he was so changed. The young man who had always seemed so lively and fun-loving was huddled in a corner like an old man with all the cares of the world on his shoulders. He was drained by both the journey and the news of Akenzader's death. With his customary lack of tact, Chris pounced on him, demanding to check the accounts. I told him to leave the poor man alone as he was exhausted and in shock from the news that had greeted his return.

That evening Roze Mohammed came into our room with a plate full of apples for Sarah and me and the three of us talked about Abdul Wahdood and how sorry we felt for him. We knew how miserable he would be if he had just to be a family man instead of being out there with his Mujahideen.

Although, in some small way, the gravity of the political situation served to unite the team, conditions in the clinic were unbearably crowded. We had been waiting so long for our house, which was progressing at a snail's pace. As the only engineer, I had taken charge of the building work, which was no easy task, especially with Chris moaning about the situation all the time. When he complained that the workers packed up whenever it rained, I pointed out that builders in Britain did exactly the same. Still, it was almost finished now, the walls were up and we could see the layout of the accommodation. The rooms ran along three sides of the courtyard with a high wall shutting off the fourth. What was to be the kitchen occupied one of the shorter sides, and the other was made up of two smaller rooms which would form the bathroom and the latrine. Along the side opposite the wall ran a long corridor which would have big windows looking out onto the courtyard and off this would be a living-room and two bedrooms, one for us women and one for Chris and Andy. Like almost all Afghan houses, it would have a flat roof supported on poplar poles. I wondered if I could prevail upon the men to give some sort of pitch to the roof, in the hope of avoiding the leaks that we had suffered in the clinic. In the end, I decided that it wasn't worth the effort of trying to persuade the Afghans to try something new. Instead, I promised myself that I would be sure to provide plenty of plastic to lay on the roof before the final layer of mud was put on.

As I wanted our house to have a supply of fresh water, I considered building a well. Abdul Wahdood had one in the courtyard of his house, so it was likely that we would hit water-bearing rock if we dug down a fair way. However, if the well was built in the courtyard, it would be too close to the latrine I was designing, and that could contaminate the well water. The ideal location was at the back of the house but, when I suggested this to Abdul Wahdood, he insisted that flash floods would come roaring down the valley and flood the well with debris. I was sceptical about this and thought the reason was more likely to be that my proposed site for the well was too close to the mosque for his liking. So, for the time being at least, I gave up the idea of having our own well. The good news was that the supplies from the bazaar that Roze Mohammed had recently returned with included the windows for our house. Once these were fitted and the roof laid, we would be able to move in.

When the day arrived, Abdul Wahdood offered his donkey to help move our trunks and equipment from the clinic to the new house. All day long the donkey went back and forth, laden with carpets, stoves, cooking equipment and tin trunks. We dashed backwards and forwards ourselves, loading at one end, unloading and sorting at the other. Once we had everything installed, we heaved a huge sigh of relief. Roze Mohammed came to tell us that the elders in the area had all gone to Abdul Wahdood and asked him to stay as commander and he had accepted. I realised how astute Abdul Wahdood was, in spite of his youth. Now he had a mandate and his position was even stronger than before Akenzader's death.

As ever, things didn't go completely smoothly. Although we welcomed the extra space, conditions in the house were far from perfect. There were trunks everywhere and it was cold and damp, as the mud walls and floor were not yet dry. The roof leaked even more than the clinic's had. Two days after we moved in, Sarah and I woke up to the sound of dripping outside our room. Water was pouring through the roof into the corridor where we'd stored several of the trunks, as well as equipment we needed for the project. We covered the trunks with plastic and put buckets under as many of the leaks as we could. Then we climbed onto the roof and started to shovel the snow off it, as this was the cause of the leak. Two of Abdul Wahdood's servants joined in, which was just as well, because it still took over an hour for the four of us to get the roof clear of snow. Exhausted from our efforts, we brewed up a pot of tea on the stove and were enjoying this when Chris stormed in. During our frantic fight with the leaks, we had failed to notice that one of his trunks, containing vital schoolbooks, had been directly beneath one of the leaks. Water had got to the contents, which were now wet through. He hurled abuse at us and it was clear that the truce established after Akenzader's death was over.

We were working flat out and the leaking roof episode showed how much we were in need of someone to help us around the house. Although we did have Abdul Garni, he was in some ways, more of a liability than an asset. He would come to our house as soon as he finished his work at the clinic, cook our lunch and evening meal and chop wood. At night he would stay on to guard us and then make tea in the morning before he went to the clinic. But after the business with my Swiss knife we knew we couldn't trust him and, sure enough, in no time at all we noticed that he'd been helping himself to the tea and coffee. He was taking more and more liberties and we didn't know how to stop him. Not only was he light-fingered, but he was also extremely uninterested in personal hygiene. It was only since we had moved to our new house that he had taken over our cooking. Almost as soon as he had taken command of the kitchen, we began to suffer from stomach problems .Also, because he was working at our house, his work at the clinic was suffering. He arrived later and later and Sarah began to think that she would have to dispense with his services. Chris and Andy were not at all keen on this idea. They'd got used to him bringing them tea in the morning and lighting their stove. However, the clinic got busier and busier and Sarah decided that she had to find another general factotum. As our money still hadn't come through, we could pay very little for this position, so Abdul Wahdood suggested Janan. He was a very poor man with only one eye and a limp. Sad to say, he was just about the ugliest man I had ever seen and, to add to his unattractiveness, it was rumoured that he had fleas.

Reluctantly, we agreed to give him a try, and at first things didn't seem too bad; the clinic returned to its old routine and Janan's cooking was perfectly edible. Then we found the lice! Sarah found them first. She had been feeling itchy and spotted the telltale eggs in her shawl. We found that all our clothes were infested. Every piece of our clothing had to be boiled. The pots bubbled away on the kitchen stove all day long, as we heaved piles of our clothes in and out of them. We hung all our bedding outside in the courtyard to be disinfected by the sun, deciding to do one side one day and then turn it over and let the other side bake the next day. Unfortunately, the weather changed yet again and I woke up to find more snow had arrived. I rushed outside and threw sheets of plastic over the mattresses and quilts to protect them from the snow.

The worst thing about the lice incident was that Sarah blamed Zebedee. She insisted that he sleep outside in the corridor and so I had to endure listening to him howling out there all night. To make matters worse he was clearly not at all well, having been sick twice and getting noticeably thinner. Despite our efforts, the lice persisted and Sarah began to accept that Zebedee couldn't be responsible. The writing was on the wall for Janan when he failed to get up one morning, so the snow didn't get cleared from the roof. As it started to melt, Chris and Andy were woken up by a steady flow of water coming in through the roof. Before they had time to do anything about it, the corner of the room collapsed, leaving them lying in bed but with a scenic view of the valley and a howling draught.

Later in the day, while we were having lunch in the workroom, water started to leak in alarmingly. Janan was up on the roof, supposedly clearing the snow, but his stomping only seemed to make things worse as before our very eyes, great lumps of mud fell into the room. Then the entire window fell out. We spent the rest of the afternoon watching helplessly, as bits of our beloved new house collapsed. Almost every room had a hole in it and the best I could do was to cut out bits of plastic to cover up the yawning gaps.

This was the last straw as far as we were concerned – Janan had to go! We went straight to Abdul Wahdood and demanded that he find us a replacement immediately. He agreed that the house collapsing was Janan's fault but he warned us that it would not be easy to find someone. I realised that one reason might be that the whole village knew by now that we'd caught lice from Janan. Janan went and, every evening, someone turned up to guard us through the night. We never knew who it was going to be, so we always had to be on our best behaviour. Apart from anything else, Sarah and I had to be sure to keep our heads covered in the house, for fear of offending one of our guardians. We also had to keep a sharp eye on all our possessions, especially kitchen utensils and cutlery, which began to disappear when Abdul Hadi spent a night or two in our kitchen.

Without any proper help, we were forced to take on all the household chores in addition to our already crowded work schedule. The task I found hardest to master was the simple act of chopping wood for the stove. I either would miss the piece altogether and come down on the hard-packed mud, sending shock waves up my back, or else the axe would embed itself in the branch and no heaving, tugging or pulling on my part would dislodge it. Finally I was forced to admit defeat and leave that job to the boys. However, I did rather well in the cooking department. Chris's watery scrambled egg and Andy's soggy mashed potatoes were no serious competition for some of the menus I conjured up. Omelette and chips, risotto and baked potatoes with tomato and onion sauce were just three of my more imaginative dishes. Baking bread also became a speciality of mine and my wholemeal bread, leavened with yeast bought in Quetta, became a favourite. It made a welcome change from the flat circles the local people produced that quickly turned into something closely resembling cardboard. It took me a few days to get used to the pressure cooker and there was a knack to getting the wood fire going, which I never grasped. I would keep on trying resolutely, staggering out of the smoke-filled kitchen every couple of minutes to gulp down a few breaths of fresh air, before diving back in again to try to master the esoteric art of keeping a wood fire going. Despite streaming eyes and choking breath, I managed somehow, and we didn't starve. The housework seemed to take up almost the whole of my day with the seemingly endless routine of fetching wood, fetching water, lighting the fire, cooking the meal and washing up. Washing up was the worst chore of all. There were no scouring pads or washing-up liquid and, although I copied the Afghans and picked up a handful of earth to scour each pot, I could never clear the dishes of grease the way the Afghans did. It was understandable when Abdul Wahdood declared that foreign women were of no value as wives. I certainly wouldn't have been able to run an Afghan household the way the local women did. Since I returned to Britain, people have often asked me how it was that the Afghans allowed Western women like myself to move around the valley and work alongside the men. I think the simple answer is that an Afghan man considers his women to have a value that must be protected. They consider that this value is decreased if other people have a sight of their women. Since we three Englishwomen were foreigners, we had no real value in their eyes and so didn't need to be protected in the same way. Thus, our moving freely about the valley was of no interest to them.

My ability as a cook was jeopardising my career as an engineer, as nobody fancied the food prepared by the others. I had no intention of spending the rest of my time in Afghanistan trapped in a smoky kitchen, so I went to Abdul Wahdood and pleaded with him to find another cook. To my relief he produced a candidate for the post within a few days, a young man called Sadiq from a family who lived on the other side of the river. Although only seventeen or eighteen, he seemed to know not only how to run a kitchen but, just as importantly, how to keep the thieves at bay. The only problem was that he wanted more pay than we had budgeted for and, until some cash arrived from Quetta, we had to watch every penny. We decided that a good cook was more important than eating meat and so instead of buying another cow we took on the new cook.

The first thing Sadiq did was to clean and tidy the kitchen. I thought I'd done reasonable job of clearing up the mess after we got rid of Janan but, after our new cook's first day or so, the place was almost unrecognisable. He put up new shelves, each one covered with a plastic sheet to keep the dust and dirt off.

He scrounged a chair for himself, which seemed only reasonable, as the kitchen was to be his home while he was working for us. We stopped eating in the workroom and joined him in the kitchen for our meals. Sadiq was keen to. try new things and soon got the hang of chips and pancakes. In the morning he would bring tea and greet us with a delightful smile that made me start the day with a light heart. Sadiq was also ingenious and, having scrounged an old speaker from one of Khodai Dahd's vehicles, he connected it to my Walkman, which had been damaged in the accident on our way into Afghanistan. Soon a steady stream of Afghan music was coming from the kitchen and, although it was not what I would have chosen for myself, it cheered the whole house up. Even Zebedee became attached to Sadiq and spent almost as much time in the kitchen as in my room.

Although we were all a good deal happier after the arrival of our expensive but talented cook, the atmosphere in the house was not permanently improved. This, of course, was mainly due to Chris. He was, unwilling to lift a hand to help anyone, yet happy to poke his nose into Sarah's accounts and pick them to pieces. He insisted on taking sole charge of the keys to our house. One night we had to wake him up because we were locked out; after that, he wasn't so keen on being 'guardian of the keys'. Slowly but surely Chris undermined Sarah's confidence as team leader. He made it clear that he felt he should be leading us and that a mere woman was unfit for the job. Sarah became withdrawn and would go for long periods without speaking. At first I put it down to her worry over the uncertain political situation surrounding Abdul Wahdood and the strain of managing the clinic without Caroline to help her. In fact, something else was on her mind. She was becoming very fond of Roze Mohammed. It was he who managed to shift her out of her lethargy. His relationship with Sarah was tempestuous and he would go on and off her, like a teenager. One of the difficulties was that he could never say 'sorry'. It wasn't that he didn't want to but he was a Pashtun, and Pashtuns never say 'sorry'. He told me he would rather have been a Hazarah, something unheard of for a Pashtun, who regard most Hazarahs as their enemies. But Hazarahs are allowed to say 'sorry'. The two of them were becoming increasingly close but, whatever their feelings might have been, it was dangerous for any woman, especially a Western woman, to get close to an Afghan, unless a marriage had been arranged.

Chris took this situation as another sign of Sarah's vulnerability and more proof that she was unfit to be the team leader. With Chris constantly berating her, Roze Mohammed's apparent romantic attachment and no money in the kitty, Sarah was at the end of her tether. Chris became more and more unpopular with the Afghans. We wanted to hold a party to celebrate moving into our new house, but several people in the village let it be known that, if Chris was going to be there, they would not come. It looked as if our party would have to wait until he had gone. Day after day he became harder to live with. He was one of the most selfish people I have ever met. If he decided to cook something for himself, it never occurred to him to do some for us. He berated the

Afghans to their faces and to us. We heaved a sigh of relief when he set off for the school in Gazak where he was to teach. However, the peace didn't last long. He was soon back, outraged that the school had used all the money he'd allocated to it for the whole winter – and we were nowhere near spring yet. Chris was convinced that money was going astray, so he went to tell Abdul Wahdood that he was going to close the school. The warlord was deeply offended, as his integrity was being called into question. He was also concerned that the school should not close, as this would undermine his standing in the area. In the end Sarah and Abdul Wahdood convinced Chris that the expenditure had been justified and could be accounted for.

The snow kept falling, Sarah got more and more depressed and Chris got more and more unbearable. I wondered how I'd survive until it was time to go. Just when I had reached the end of my tether, there was a ray of hope. Jelahd Khan, one of the outreach workers, arrived from Quetta. He had waited behind with Abdul Hamid to help transport the trees, the funding for my irrigation project and, just as importantly, Caroline, back from Pakistan. Although he arrived empty-handed, with no news of Caroline or the money, he was able to tell me about the trees. They were on their way, but had been snowed in en route. One of the trusted helpers had stayed with the trees and would bring them on to Daichopan the moment the weather changed. Jelahd Khan had also brought a bundle of letters. That lifted my spirits and I read them avidly. After living in the valley for so long, cut off from the outside world, it was wonderful to have news from home; I learnt that Nelson Mandela had been freed and the Berlin wall demolished. Two of the most important world events in my lifetime and here was I, marooned far from newspapers or television.

The letters only served to lift my spirits for a short time. I felt cut off from the world and, for the first time since coming to Afghanistan, I was homesick. I was stuck in one of the world's most primitive countries with a clinically depressed midwife and a power-crazed teacher. Not ideal – and where was my money? Where was Caroline?

Chapter Eight

The snows melted and winter was at last making way for spring. My spirits lifted, as the nights grew less cold and the days warmer. However, I was worried about my cat, Zebedee, as he had lost a lot of his usual bounce. He had never fully recovered from being shut outside in the cold during the lice episode. He got thinner and thinner and his beautiful tiger-striped coat started to look mangy. I knew something was seriously wrong with him; he would sit shivering on my lap, even if the room was warm. I knew virtually nothing about cats, so I felt powerless, but it occurred to me that he might be suffering from worms. One day, when he was shivering even more than usual, he walked into the kitchen stove. I spotted this in the nick of time and snatched him away before he could burn himself too severely. But he was singed down one side and lost all the fur from his tail. I asked Sarah to let me have a de-worming tablet. Now these were designed for humans and I had no idea what effect they might have on a cat, so I cut it into quarters and crushed one of these pieces into some meat for Zebedee. Within days his condition had noticeably improved and in less than a week he was his old bouncing self again. As we had decided that we couldn't afford any more meat, the piece I gave the cat his tablet in was our last. Keeping meat was impossible anyway; there was nowhere dry in our house and it soon grew maggots and became inedible.

Then came my first piece of really good news. My trees had arrived, or very nearly. They were stored at the village of Kharnai, not many miles away, and I was needed there to check and count them. But the atmosphere in our area was far from tranquil. Perhaps because the political situation, with Abdul Wahdood still not assured of his position, many of the Afghans were nervous and particularly vigilant. Armed men slept in the clinic and on the mountain above it, ready to ward off attackers.

I set off for Kharnai to look at my trees, with Khodai Mir as my bodyguard. He was jumpy and kept entreating me to keep up with him. Sleepless nights guarding the clinic had made him short-tempered and nervous. At Kharnai, I found Roze Mohammed sitting amongst piles of saplings, which were wrapped up in straw and sacking, each bundle carefully labelled. I was greatly relieved to see my trees at last: they included apples, almonds, peaches and pears. Roze Mohammed said that he had counted them all and that, of the original 14,000 saplings expected, 5,000 were missing! I thought it was miraculous that so many had arrived intact as, with the hold-up in the snow and other delays, they had been en route from Quetta for about two months.

While I was checking the saplings I received some very welcome news. Caroline had arrived back in the valley. Leaving Roze Mohammed in charge, I went back to our house as fast as I could and, behold, there she was. We exchanged big hugs and kisses and she handed me a present – an orange – the first fresh vitamin C I'd had for months. Caroline produced another and far more exciting present – 2,000 dollars in local currency to pay for the renovation of the irrigation system at Gazak. What a day! My trees, my money, my friend – and an orange!

There was no time for relaxing as Chris was departing for Quetta the next day and I had to complete reports and letters for him to take back. I was pleased that I had been able to report the safe arrival of the trees and, as Chris started off in the early-morning light, I breathed a sigh of relief. Perhaps, with him gone, there would be some peace and harmony. There was no time to dwell on the joys of life without Chris though; shortly after his departure, the camels arrived with Caroline's luggage and the extra supplies she had brought from Quetta. While we were busy unloading, I noticed Sarah and Roze Mohammed disappeared into our house. When Caroline went inside to sort out the contents of her trunk, she heard the couple in deep conversation in our room. Not wanting to disturb them, she came out again and we completed the unpacking of supplies. It was dusk before Roze Mohammed emerged looking serious, followed by a very subdued Sarah. I didn't pay them too much attention, as my thoughts were occupied with my trip down to Kharnai the next day, where I was going to hand out the trees. Later, when it was dark, I found Sarah sitting on a wall staring into space. She refused to talk about Roze Mohammed, so I decided to let it rest for the moment and devote all my energies to distributing thousands of little trees to the deserving landowners.

Not unusually for Afghanistan, there was a mix-up the next morning about my departure for Kharnai. I was ready to leave at dawn but Mullah Ahmed Zai, who was to accompany me, was waiting at Abdul Wahdood's house, having misunderstood as usual. This put me in such a bad mood that I started off without him, leaving him to catch up as best he could. We got to Kharnai at about eight o'clock in the morning and I started to sort out the different kinds of trees, with help from Khodai Mir. I was still hard at it when hordes of people started to arrive. We had calculated that there were enough trees for each household in the valley to have fourteen. They were all to receive the same mix of red and yellow apples, almonds and pears. The next eight hours were a mad rush, as we handed out hundreds and hundreds of saplings, making sure to get a thumbprint from each householder as a sign that they had received their allowance of trees. There was no chance of signatures in a country with about ninety per cent illiteracy.

We struggled to make order out of chaos, Mullah Ahmed Zai sitting amongst the piles of saplings, behaving like a demented mother hen, clucking at everyone in sight and having a wonderful time. Khodai Mir scribbled madly, as names were called out and he checked them against his list. I had charge of the ink-pad and collected thumbprints alongside the list of names I had prepared. My main concern was to ensure that I had as accurate a record as possible, so that I could present it as evidence to the UN that their money had been well spent.

Once the trees had been distributed I could concentrate on the building of the bridge, one of my prime reasons for coming to this valley. I had been in Daichopan for some six months and one delay after another had prevented me from even starting. Most of the delays were caused by the local residents' inability to agree a site for the bridge. One landowner after another declared that he didn't want other people's cattle walking across his land. It began to look as if this wrangling would go on indefinitely, in which case I would never get my bridge built. Then, as the snows melted and spring approached, the river level rose at an alarming rate. The river flowed with greater and greater force until, one morning, the existing bridge by the clinic was swept clean away. Everyone's minds became wonderfully focused. Abdul Wahdood in particular gave his undivided attention to the problem and came up with a site for the bridge that seemed acceptable to all parties. The only drawback was that this favoured location was at a particularly wide part of the river. This was not at all the best place for the bridge from an engineering point of view. However, the location had been unanimously decided by the local residents and that was a first!

Another problem I'd been wrestling with for some time was finding suitable trees to form the beams of the bridge. I had given Abdul Wahdood 20,000 Afghanis (about £20), which he said was the price of two tall trees he would get from a place called Khak Iran. This was the highest part of Daichopan, way out beyond Gazak where apparently the best stands of poplars were to be found. Chris had asked about the trees when he visited Gazak but nobody had seemed to know anything about them, which seemed strange. Abdul Wahdood had assured me that there was a difficulty in finding suitably seasoned wood but Chris had been convinced that the man had just pocketed the money. At first I thought this was just Chris being Chris, but now I began to wonder. Poplar trees were everywhere in the area, so how hard could it be to find a couple of good, big, strong tree trunks? However, when Abdul Wahdood gave his undivided attention to something he did get results. Just as a decision had been reached about the location of the bridge when it became vital to do so, so two suitable poplar trees were suddenly located in Alu, just a short walk from the clinic. I was taken to view them before they were cut down and they looked magnificent. As I watched them being felled, I realised how sheltered from reality we are in our modern life. Trees are being cut down all the time to provide furniture, paper and other goods for our everyday lives and we rarely give it a second thought. But now I was deeply moved at seeing these giants of the forest, that had taken decades to mature, brought down in a few minutes. Once felled, the trees were hauled to the river site by four powerful oxen. Now I had the beams for my bridge, but I was also going to need supports and piers. To provide heavy, immovable foundations beneath the water we had to create gabions. These are large wire baskets, constructed by weaving thick strands of wire skilfully together. These baskets are filled with heavy rocks and thus the bridge's structure has something firm to stand on. I found two men who had worked in Iran and knew how to weave the wire for gabions. One of these was called Kharnor; I was particularly pleased to be able to give him work as his family were so friendly, calling out to us as we passed them on our daily walk between our house and the clinic. Kharnor's wife, Barakzi, was not well and, to add to their troubles, half their house had collapsed during a heavy snowstorm and Kharnor had talked of going to work in Pakistan to earn enough money to rebuild his house. I hoped the money from the gabion-making would enable him to stay, as Barakzi would not be able to manage the house and the fields on her own.

As both men insisted they knew all about making gabions, I gave them a large coil of wire and some tools each and left them to make a start. I had tried my hand at gabion-making, based on what little I had read and observed, and was interested to see how it should be done. They each adopted a different method, which were both quite unlike mine. I had my doubts about Menai's ability. He worked quickly but with a very open mesh that did not look strong or rigid. I felt he should have been paid less than Kharnor but the deal had been struck. I put my foot down when Abdul Wahdood suggested that Menai should build more than Kharnor because he worked more quickly. I could not help feeling that the fact that Menai was Abdul Wahdood's cousin had something to do with this suggestion.

As the weather grew warmer the river continued to rise. The snow showers had been replaced by rain and snow now lay only in the shaded places beneath the trees and on the upper slopes of the mountains. A white mist hovered round each of the almond trees, as the blossom slowly opened. The rapidly rising river was not going to make my job any easier and I wished that we had been able to complete the job the previous autumn, when the water had been only a few feet deep. Now I was faced with a rushing, brown, turbulent flood whose depth was difficult to gauge. As Chris and Andy had brought my surveying level out with them, I was able to measure the distance across the river quite easily. I sent Khodai Mir across to the other side with the level staff, while I took readings surrounded by a cluster of curious Afghans, clamouring for a chance to look through the telescope. Khodai Mir was adept at using the level; he explained that it was not much different from using a gun sight. Perhaps he was smarter than I had given him credit for.

Once I had measured the distance across the river I was able to design the bridge. I persuaded Abdul Wahdood to move the location about fifty yards down river, which reduced the width a little. We would still have to build a very long bridge with three spans. Even so, at times people might have to wade through shallow water to reach the bridge, if the river came up very high. Two of the spans would rest on three supports built out of gabions. This would extend the bridge across the flood plain, which was already several inches deep in water and could become even deeper. The longest span would reach from the far bank to the edge of the main channel of the river. But the river level had become so high that I could not follow my original plan. It would not be possible to use gabions as the supports for the main span, as the tree trunks were not long enough to reach to the shallow area. We would need to make a taller support in the form of a wooden trestle, which the men called a 'donkey'. It would consist of two A-frames, joined at the top by a cross-member, resembling the four legs and back of a donkey. I had seen similar structures used to protect the riverbank so I was confident that the local workers would be able to make one. The extra spans and the donkey meant that I had to buy more trees, which involved negotiating with prospective vendors, an exercise that took hours of haggling and endless cups of tea. It may not have been as convenient as the builders' merchant back home but it was much more fun, and I had now become used to the slower pace of life in Afghanistan. The building of the new bridge took on greater urgency with each passing day for, as the water level grew higher and higher, so it became more and more difficult to put the construction in place. Despite this pressure, I found unsuspected resources of patience, and accepted the need to spend hours in Abdul Wahdood's guest room discussing who would offer what trees and at what price, as we drank the familiar black tea in the equally familiar small fluted glasses. At last the deals were struck and the trees were delivered the next day.

At the same time as thinking about the building of the new bridge, I had to work out how best to spend the money Caroline had delivered for work on the irrigation scheme up at Gazak. My main difficulty was communication. With the original bridge washed away, it was virtually impossible to meet with anyone from Gazak, as they would have to make a detour of many miles to get across to my side of the river, something they weren't willing to do. For myself, I couldn't spare the time to go up there with the journey time now doubled. Mullah Ahmed Zai tried tying letters around rocks and hurling them across the river to us but this was hardly an effective way of carrying out a complex dialogue, so we gave it up. For the same reason, it was practically impossible to supervise the building of the support for the bridge on the far side. I was forced to leave the people from the village of Band Killay, on the other side of the river, to their own devices. Nevertheless, I was able to watch them hard at work and I realised how cut off they must have felt from the main centre of control in the valley.

I found myself becoming frustrated at the leisurely pace of progress on my side of the river. The river was still rising and yet very little was being done. Although work had begun on the building of the donkey, there were only a couple of men working for two or three hours a day on the project. My frustration grew when I found that the saplings, which we had planted around the clinic to provide both shade and fruit, had been dug up and stolen during the night. There were times when the place began to drive me mad with its constant air of lethargy. In no time at all it would be Ramadan, and then I'd be hard pressed to get any work out of anyone for about a month. The catch was that, until the bridge was completed, I couldn't get up to Gazak to do any work there, so I had to try to exercise patience, knowing that my departure date was drawing ever closer. The thought of having to leave the valley before any of my projects were completed was heartbreaking.

The one bright spot in my life at this time was the arrival in the valley of a tinsmith. At last I could get the water containers repaired that had been damaged when our lorry crashed on our journey into the valley. It was fascinating watching this man hammering the metal as he carefully heated it over a small charcoal fire. His soldering iron had to be heated on the fire, but he seemed quite as expert with it as any craftsman back in England. Once the water containers were repaired I would be able to set up a proper filter for the clinic and that would improve their water quality no end. Filling a tin tank with sand, I allowed water to percolate over it. A layer of charcoal across the top improved the taste and the water, when we drained off the clean, clear liquid from a tap at the bottom, tasted wonderfully fresh. A far cry from the not so clean stuff we had been taking straight from the stream.

While I waited for progress on the bridge, I found myself co-opted into other roles. One day I assisted Caroline and Sarah with an operation on a young girl. They were working in the kitchen and called out for me to bring a bowl. When I walked in with it, I was passed another bowl full of blood and asked to dispose of it. I was surprised how well I dealt with this, considering that I'd never been able to stand the sight of blood. I found myself able to carry on as their assistant, passing surgical instruments to them and removing more bowls of blood. The girl had been brought to Caroline complaining of pains in her stomach. Although in her mid-teens, she had never had a period; her hymen had blocked the entrance to her uterus completely, so that none of her monthly bleeding had been able to escape. I felt pleased that I had been able to help, albeit in a very minor role. Caroline and I got on much better after this, although the reason may have been that she was beginning to appreciate that my job could be just as tiring and frustrating as hers. She didn't have to stand for long hours in the rain and haul gabions around. Perhaps we all got on better now that Chris wasn't there.

Now that the atmosphere in the house was so much improved, we decided to hold a housewarming. Abdul Hadi helped Sadiq with the cooking and they produced a veritable feast of rice, stew and chicken. We even had some after-dinner mints, which had been sent out to Sarah from England. When we passed these round, they were much appreciated by the Afghans, who love sweet things. Abdul Wahdood was at the party; I asked for his help in getting the bridge finished. When we met the next morning, I explained the problem and he suggested that I should pay some of the local men to work on the bridge. There was no way I was going to agree to that. The people of Daichopan wanted this bridge. They would have built a replacement one, whatever happened. Eventually we reached a compromise. No one would be paid for building a basic bridge, but if I wanted to improve it then I would pay for the extra work. I intended to have a proper deck with handrails, so that women would not be afraid to cross the bridge, so I knew that sooner or later some of the workers would have to be paid. It seemed a reasonable deal to me. Abdul Wahdood wrote to all the villages on our side of the river and the next day a crowd of people arrived. Work was beginning in earnest.

Unfortunately they had chosen the coldest and wettest day for weeks to start serious work. The rain came down in sheets and I was thankful for my Gore-Tex waterproof jacket. The Afghans only had their patous to fend off the cold and rain. The steel wire of the gabions was dragged down the river bank and positioned in the water. A human chain was formed to pass rocks from the land to fill up the wire gabions. I had to stand up to my knees in the freezing water to direct the work. It wasn't long before I lost all feeling in my feet. The cold spread up my entire body, until I felt chilled to the bone. Eventually, allowing for the usual stops for prayers, the gabion was filled, the wire lid attached and tied down. The structure looked more like a lump of grey blancmange than the neat rectangular blocks I had seen back home but it felt quite solid. We decided to call it a day and the Afghans lit a fire to get warm. I wished I could get a fire to light the way they could. It looked so easy, but I still had frequent struggles with the stove in our room. Luckily, with the weather turning a little warmer, we didn't need it every night now. The Afghans huddled round the fire and dried off the ends of their trousers. I suddenly had a brainwave and, rushing back to our house, grabbed a huge bar of chocolate that the director of REDR had sent me. It was just big enough for everyone to have a piece and I hoped it would encourage them to turn up again tomorrow.

Whether because of the chocolate or, more likely, the command from Abdul Wahdood, the villagers did indeed turn up the next morning, and three more gabions were filled. Two supports were completely finished and only one more gabion was needed to complete the task. That left the donkey, which had been built on shore, to be manoeuvred in place by workers in the water. By now this was three or four feet deep with a strong current. Several of the local people stripped off completely apart from their patous, the shawls they wore most of the time, which they tied around their waists. 'Most un-Islamic', I thought, inwardly admiring Sadiq's physique. A rope was tied to the donkey, and it was hauled into the water. Several of the people in the water were having difficulty keeping their feet in the fast-flowing river; I prayed that none of them would be swept away. At one point it looked as though the entire structure might topple over and be carried off by the current but somehow they got it into position. Placing the long poplar poles for the main span proved almost as difficult as getting the donkey in place. The beams had to be fed out across the supports at our end, hauled by ropes from the far bank. Once they were in place, I heaved a sigh of relief that my calculations had been correct: that the poles were indeed long enough. There was no way I was going to let everyone rest on their laurels, so I insisted that the cross-members be nailed to the beams to make proper decking. Then I fixed uprights to each support with wire strung between them, thus providing steadying handholds for anyone crossing the bridge. Menai and Kharnor, who carried out the work, were very scathing about it. 'Why do we need to do all this?' they asked. I explained that as women rarely left their homes, if they came to the clinic via the bridge they may not be accustomed to crossing a bridge, but they were not convinced. I wasn't sure whether this was because they thought women could cross a bridge as easily as men or because they could not imagine any women being allowed so far from their houses. I knew I had been right to insist when I later helped Roze Mohammed's mother, Kaptara, across the bridge. She clung to the wire handholds – 'This good bridge', she said to me.

The bridge was finished. My grand design had been achieved. It was wonderful to see people crossing back and forth on what I considered to be a rather elegant construction. I had another plan to bring to fruition, not so ambitious as the bridge but radical just the same. Caroline, Sarah and I would invite Kaptara and Barakzi to tea. As a dai, or wise woman, Kaptara had been working with Sarah. Barakzi was the wife of Kharnor, who lived between the clinic and our house. It was revolutionary for unrelated women to meet at the house of some foreigners. We planned the party for a Friday when we'd be on our own. Sadiq would be at his own house and Andy was going to spend a few days in Abqol. Sarah made some Earl Grey tea and, as well as producing my last block of chocolate, I baked some bread. Kaptara and Barakzi arrived and we sat by the large window in the outer veranda of our house with the spring sunshine streaming in. At first they were both a little shy but, before long, we were gossiping away. One of the topics was Roze Mohammed. When would he get married? What could Barakzi do to cure her youngest child's lingering cough? What would we do when we returned to England? A shadow was cast over our happy tea party, when Barakzi told us she was pregnant.

Under Islamic law, a man can have more than one wife. As far as most men are concerned, a woman's chief function is to bear him sons; women in the area around us generally had a pregnancy every year. Barakzi was no exception and was worn out. She had borne Kharnor twelve children, of whom only five had survived. After the latest birth she had haemorrhaged continuously for two months; Sarah and Caroline agreed this was purely due to the repeated pregnancies. It could be fatal for her to have another baby before her body had been given proper time to recover. Sarah had suggested that she should go on the Pill but she refused to make any decision about it herself: we would have to discuss it with Kharnor. We were all invited to dinner. The meal was very convivial and we chatted about daily events while tucking in to a delicious stew of quail, provided by Kharnor, whose skill as a hunter was known throughout the valley. When the meal was over, tea was served and it was time to broach the subject of the Pill. Caroline explained to Kharnor that it would be best for Barakzi if they waited for a year before having any more children. He answered that if Barakzi could not have a child the following year he would take a second wife. Barakzi told us that she would then be relegated to drudgery, doing the housework and supporting the new wife. So it was that Barakzi refused contraception and two months later we heard what we had been dreading – she was pregnant again. This made me very angry, but what made me even more angry was that Kharnor declared that he could not afford another child unless he went away to work in Iran. If only he had gone away sooner his wife would have been able to take the necessary rest and been ready to bear him another child when he returned. As it was she would be left on her own when she was already dangerously sick. To try to overcome this problem, Barakzi and her family moved away to stay with relatives, but we never heard what became of her.

Now that I had a bridge, I could get up to Gazak. If I didn't go soon, the spring floods would make work on repairing the irrigation systems impossible. Ramadan was approaching and that could make all work extremely difficult. Just days before the old bridge was washed away, Abdul Wahdood had called a meeting of representatives from the Gazak area to discuss the work to be done. For two days the men sat outside Abdul Wahdood's house arguing at the tops of their voices. I asked him what the outcome of all this chatter had been and he explained the hold-up. Mullah Ahmed Zai had prepared a list of the work to be included in the project but had been in his house in Gazak when the old bridge had been washed away. Now that he was no longer marooned but had a brand new bridge to cross to us, we were awaiting his arrival. When he did turn up, he'd left the vital list of works at his house and had to go all the way back to get it. Whilst we waited for him, I explained to Abdul Wahdood how I planned to carry out the project. I would visit all the sites where work was to be undertaken and agree what work was required. I would then revisit them later to inspect the finished work. Abdul Wahdood looked worried but I assumed that this was because Mullah Ahmed Zai still had not returned.

When Mullah Ahmed Zai returned with the list of works, he explained what he'd written but it meant nothing to me. I needed to see the actual locations, so I asked Abdul Wahdood how soon I could get up there. The warlord's answer was 'Soon', which I took to mean within the next few days. Over the next few days I kept asking him the same question and got the same answer each time, 'Soon'. At this rate I would never get to Gazak and the project money, brought all that way at such risk by Caroline, would have to be returned.

I felt greatly frustrated at the delay in getting to Gazak, but there were other things to occupy my mind. One of the Mujahideen arrived with letters from Chris. He had told many of the staff in the UN offices in Quetta that the project was a complete disaster, with stealing and financial irregularities. Health Unlimited had written to say they were sending an independent monitor to assess the project. We felt nervous about the news; what would they think of the work in Daichopan? I was very aware of my lack of experience and wondered how my projects would be regarded. Chris had also informed UNILOG (the specialist transport section of the UN) that some of my trees had gone missing, so they were demanding to know where they were. Khodai Mir had compiled a list when I was handing out the trees in Kharnai. For some reason it had been passed to Mullah Ahmed Zai but, when I asked him for it, he had to go all the way back to his house to get it. I was losing patience with the Mullah: he never seemed to be in the right place at the right time with the right information. He was also proving impossible to teach English to. He had still not progressed beyond, 'I have a mother and a father'. Khodai Mir could now speak some quite passable, although rudimentary, English. The problem with the Mullah wasn't just his complete lack of English. He seemed to find it impossible to master the simplest techniques, and he still couldn't even read a tape measure. One way and another, he was not an ideal assistant.

The Mullah never did find one of his sheets of paper but fortunately I had made my own list when the trees were being checked, so I was able to go through this with Abdul Wahdood. We checked and double-checked and, as far as we could see, all the trees had been correctly handed out. However, there were indeed five hundred others not accounted for. The person who might know was Abdul Hamid, but he was not in a co-operative mood. He had asked Sarah for extra money to cover what he claimed were additional expenses while he was in Quetta. She considered that the daily allowance he had been given was quite sufficient. Thus there existed a stand-off, and now the man was nowhere to be found. I had to solve the mystery of the disappearing trees in the few weeks that were left before my reports had to be with the UN.

Having worked hard to galvanise everyone in the area into building the new bridge, I found that it no longer held any interest for the local population.

I wasn't happy about the wooden donkey supporting the structure. It needed to be strengthened before the rising water became more forceful, when it might topple the whole structure over. There were some gabions that had not been used which could be placed around the donkey support and secured with wire. When I asked Abdul Wahdood to organise some more workers for this job the question of money was immediately raised. I hated the continual arguments over money. We had virtually run out of money and could not pay anyone, whether we wanted to or not. It was their bridge and had been built for their benefit so, if they wanted a bridge, then they'd have to get on and do the necessary work without any payment.

No one knew exactly when Ramadan would start. Somewhere a group of mullahs was watching the moon each night and they would say when it started. One evening, as we were having our meal in the kitchen, we heard the sound of gunfire and Sadiq informed us that this was the signal that Ramadan had begun. Sarah, Caroline and I had agreed that we would also observe it, not so much as a sign of respect for the local people, but as a way of judging whether the Afghans were using it as an excuse to slack off or whether working and keeping Ramadan really was tough. It would mean having nothing to eat or drink during daylight hours, which were reckoned to be from four in the morning to six in the evening.

On that first night, we were woken up at two in the morning so that we could have peshlomay, the early-morning meal that was the last we were allowed until dusk the next evening. I pulled on my dress and staggered to the kitchen. Sadiq had cooked a superb stew with rice but it was difficult to digest at a time when my system thought it should be fast asleep. I wondered which was going to be worse – having only one meal a day or suffering from sleep deprivation because of having this crazy dinner at two in the morning. We found a way of coping by buying yoghurt from Barakzi and persuading Sadiq that this, with a little rice, was a more suitable way for us women to start a long day of fasting. We seemed to handle Ramadan much better than most of the Afghans. Sadiq usually overslept in spite of a giant alarm clock beside his bed, and Caroline often arrived at the clinic to find a bunch of health workers curled up asleep on the floor.

It was interesting to observe the different reactions to our keeping Ramadan. Some people were pleased that we were observing their customs, others couldn't understand why we would voluntarily do something that they hated and would have avoided if they could. Some local people thought the idea of non-Muslims keeping Ramadan was blasphemous. Our answer was to quote the Christian observance of Lent, when everyone is supposed to give up something they like for forty days. We argued that eating and drinking during the working day was what we were giving up for Lent. I suspected that some of the Afghans got angry partly because our observance of Ramadan dented their religious superiority. They believed that Islam was the true religion and that they were the elite of the world. In fact, my ability to cope with fasting and working was to be severely tested over the coming weeks.

Chapter Nine

D espite observing Ramadan, it was becoming urgent for me to make a trip up to Gazak. The work on restoring the irrigation systems there couldn't begin until I was present to agree with the people in Gazak what needed to be done. I now had the money for the project, which Caroline had brought back from Quetta. If we left it any longer, the spring rains would make it impossible to complete the work before my scheduled return to England. I was expecting Khodai Mir to be my guide and bodyguard on the trip up to Gazak, but he kept saying that he couldn't go. His excuses were feeble but I couldn't work out what the real problem was. Then I discovered that it was all to do with Mullah Ahmed Zai.

As far as I was concerned, the Mullah had become an increasing liability. He couldn't, or wouldn't, learn English, which made him useless as an interpreter. Every time I needed a document from him, it was either lost or in the wrong place. Finally, he stretched my patience to breaking point and so, as they say in the corporate world, I had to 'let him go'. I simply told him that I would no longer be requiring his services. Back in England this might have been a sufficient way of terminating his employment, but not in this case. The Mullah had family in Gazak, where he was very well known and much respected. Khodai Mir didn't feel that he could accompany me to Gazak if the Mullah was no longer working for me. It would be too shaming for Ahmed Zai if his friends and family saw that I had fired him. Realising that some diplomacy was required, I came up with a solution whereby everyone could save face. Mullah Ahmed Zai could come to Gazak with me, but I wouldn't pay him. He could do what he wanted up there and I wouldn't tell anyone that he wasn't still working for me. Honour would be preserved, but there would be no one to help me who knew about the karezes. Despite this, I was determined to go without Mullah Ahmed Zai hindering me at every turn and, as luck would have it, I was to find the support I needed when I got there.

When I told Abdul Wahdood what I was proposing he smiled admiringly.

'You are a very clever woman', he said. He admitted rather shamefacedly, that the landowners up at Gazak had already presented him with a list of works they claimed to have done and were demanding payment for them. That was why he had seemed concerned when I first described how I would work. I was pretty sure that only routine maintenance would have been carried out and I certainly wasn't paying for that. I had to initiate the work and see it carried out to my specification before I was prepared to make any payment. The warlord didn't think the landowners would take too kindly to my marching up there and telling them that in so many words. He thought my life might well be in danger if I did have the nerve to try it. I wasn't convinced and suspected that Abdul Wahdood was afraid of losing face. His position of power in the area was still very insecure since the death of this father, the all-powerful Akenzader. For days we talked the problem over, but at least we were able to talk. With so many of the Afghans that I had met there was nothing but blustering, sulking and never an agreement reached. Finally we made some progress. I pointed out that lots of farmers in Gazak would have plans they would like to implement if only they had the money. As no work, other than that routinely carried out by them, had yet been done, no one was out of pocket. Therefore, if some of my work was carried out by the very people who were demanding money, I would be able to pay them and honour would be satisfied all round. Abdul Wahdood loved the idea. So much that he announced, 'You will go to Gazak tomorrow!' I had been waiting for weeks to go there and now that I'd come up with a solution, I had to go the very next day.

This was typical warlord behaviour and it left me only a matter of hours to hammer out my monthly report for UNDP and get my things together for the journey. But at least I was going.

On the way to Gazak we were joined by three young men, brothers of Nur Rajan, who had been working in Pakistan. One of them had a cassette player that he had bought there, so we had Afghan music all the way along our journey. We were quite a jolly band, laughing and joking as we went. I found the climb much more exhausting than on my previous trip up there as, in observing Ramadan, I wasn't able to drink anything during the daytime.

As we arrived on the high plateau of Gazak, a small boy spotted us and returned within minutes with a huge crowd of children. They made a great fuss of the young men returning from Pakistan but they also gave me something of a hero's welcome, which surprised me. By the time we reached Nur Rajan's house, it seemed the entire village had turned out to greet us. Although my Pashtu was still very limited, I was pleased to discover that I could hold a reasonable conversation with Nur Rajan's wife. I enquired after her health and that of her baby and learnt that my hero's welcome was because everyone thought that I was bringing work and wages to the area, especially the young men who had shared our journey up to Gazak. They had come back from Pakistan on the understanding that there was to be paid work for them in Gazak. I could have chatted with her all day but we had to start a tour of all the villages in the area to check out the karezes there. Khodai Mir pointed out that he didn't know his way around Gazak, and I certainly didn't. I wondered if I had been too hasty in firing Mullah Ahmed Zai; at least he knew his way around the area. I needn't have worried, for Nur Rajan offered his help. It was not the first or the last time that he helped me out of a tricky situation.

As we travelled around we saw some karezes that still had water flowing but many were either blocked or emitting only a thin trickle. By evening I was exhausted, having hardly stopped all day. I'd clambered up and down the steep hills of the area, looking at the sparkling water flowing from the karezes without being able to drink a single drop. It had been torture. As soon as it was officially sundown, I was allowed a drink and knelt at a karez to gulp the water as it flowed out of the hillside. I had never tasted anything so good in all my life. It was cool and refreshing and I immediately felt better. I was led to one of the farmer's houses and fed on greasy scrambled eggs, which for once tasted delicious. Almost anything would have tasted good after a heavy day's work on no food. I gulped down more water from a container on the table and hoped it was from a hill spring and not some polluted stream.

I spent the night at Nur Rajan's house, but I was woken at two o'clock in the morning for the worst meal of my life. It consisted of tasteless, gritty bread that seemed to have had sand added to the flour in its baking, accompanied by boiled mutton fat that made me gag on every mouthful. The meal would have been intolerable at the best of times but, served at 2 am, it was impossible to stomach. Noticing that I wasn't eating, Nur Rajan's wife chided me for not getting a good meal inside me before a hard day's work. I told her that I just wasn't used to eating that early and hoped she would understand and not be offended. I knew they were very poor and that she had provided the best meal she could. The only sustenance I had that day was the sugary tea that followed the disgusting early breakfast. I drank as much as I could, in the hope that it would go some way towards preparing me for another day without food or drink. Why had I undertaken to go on such a rigorous fast when I knew I was going to be climbing up hill and down dale for days on end?

At daybreak Mullah Ahmed Zai turned up and, refusing to accept that he had been fired, hurried me off to view several karezes that I'd seen the day before. He gave me information that was completely different from what the owners of the land had told me. Once again I made it clear to the Mullah that he was wasting my time and that he was no longer in my employ. It was like banging my head against a brick wall. What I wanted was a meeting with all the landowners to discuss a schedule of works. This was arranged with help from Nur Rajan and Abdul Wahid, the health worker who was running the local clinic. When

I got to the local school, where the meeting was to take place, the representatives from one of the villages had failed to show up. Abdul Wahid suggested I wait for a while, in the hope that they would eventually arrive, and said that I could watch the local children playing 'muj'games. The teachers organised the children into two groups. One set of children were the ground forces, armed with tree branches to represent rocket launchers and anti-aircraft guns while on the ridge above them the others, representing aircraft, sought to 'bomb' the ground forces and avoid being shot down. It sent a shiver down my spine. How would they ever stop fighting with this sort of training so young?

When everyone was present, the meeting began; they all wanted to know why I hadn't been up to Gazak sooner. Abdul Wahid acted as interpreter, although I was able to explain most things myself. I reminded them of how busy I'd been on the building of the bridge, something of benefit to them all. The twenty or so Afghan landowners sat in stony-faced silence whilst I read out a list of different types of work to be undertaken. I, a Western woman, was telling these tough Muslim men what they were going to do. With the help of Abdul Wahdood I had worked out what I considered to be a fair price for each job. Everyone wanted to haggle and argue over the suggested wages but, eventually, everything was settled. I told them that I would only pay for work that I had agreed to in advance. Each piece of work would have to be personally measured by me and I would not pay anyone in Gazak; they would have to come to our house in Bitow for their money. There was no way that I was going to wander around in the hills of Afghanistan with a load of cash on me – I might not last five minutes.

On the way back we stopped to inspect yet more karezes and I thought how wonderful it would be if only I could take the tiniest drink from one of them. I could quite see how wanderers in the desert are reputed to go mad from thirst. Everything else about the journey was wonderful. The weather was glorious, with warm sun and clear, mountain air. The fields were bright green with the newly sprouted wheat and small tulips flowered in crevices amongst the rocks. Along the way, Khodai Mir borrowed a donkey for me. It was a kind thought, but I soon found out donkeys and I are just not made for each other. They don't have reins or stirrups like horses; you just sit on them, while they pick their way along the path. I had no idea where the path went and so, when the donkey suddenly changed direction I, unfortunately, did not. After falling off several times, I was happy to hand the donkey over to Khodai Mir, who rode the beast all the way back.

When I got home, I found Sarah still very subdued. Caroline told me that, although she'd spent most of the night sitting outside the house with her, she'd not been able to get to the truth of her depression. Several of the locals had observed the two women outside the house after dark and had reported this 'unseemly' behaviour to Abdul Wahdood, who had become very angry. Two of his 'English ladies' had let him down in the eyes of his people. Later that day it became clear that Caroline and Sarah were no longer in favour with him when we received the news that Abdul Wahdood's stepmother, one of Akenzader's wives, had died. We were concerned that neither Sarah nor Caroline had been called to see the old lady before she died, a clear indication that all was not well between them and the warlord. We prayed that the situation would not deteriorate further.

The stepmother's funeral was a small affair compared to the grand send-off for Akenzader. However, the new bridge was a boon, as many of the people attending came from the other side of the valley. Everyone had the day off but, as it was Ramadan, Abdul Wahdood didn't have to provide a feast, something he must have been thankful for after the huge expense of his father's funeral. The next day he summoned Sarah and Caroline to a meeting to admonish them for the seemingly innocuous act of sitting outside their own house after dark. We felt that this was only part of the story and that, with his power over the valley still in doubt, he was probably nervous at the thought of the imminent arrival of a monitor to assess the project. If it were closed down it would be a disastrous blow to the young warlord's prestige in the area. Things

132

seemed to be falling apart around us. First, Sadiq, our excellent cook, gave notice and then Abdul Wahdood's right-hand man, Roze Mohammed, disappeared on a trip to the bazaar, taking not only his jeep but also his youngest brother, without asking. Then Caroline caught Abdul Garni red-handed stealing medicines from the clinic. She had long suspected him but, until then, had been able to prove nothing. Worst of all, Abdul Wahdood received an extraordinary letter from a group of mullahs in Abqol complaining about my behaviour. They accused me of playing games with the men, going up into the mountains with them and laughing at their women. I had, in fact, laughed with their women, not at them. Abdul Wahdood said he would try to get a ruling from a more senior mullah that my actions were not un-Islamic. In the meantime Sarah, Caroline and I were not to visit Abqol. My frustration with the local people was mounting, as I couldn't persuade anyone to do the necessary work to strengthen the bridge, and the fierce spring waters were already threatening its safety. Things were now so uncomfortable that I was glad I would shortly have to go back up to Gazak to check on the work being carried out there.

I nearly didn't go up to Gazak again. The water level of the river rose rapidly, after several days of rain. I pleaded with Abdul Wahdood to get the bridge strengthened with more gabions. A few days later, Sarah told me that she had seen people working on the bridge and I hurried there to have a look. To my horror I saw that they had dismantled my gabions and were using the wire to try to fix stones on top of the trestle. This was crazy, so I immediately sought out Abdul Wahdood and let him have the full force of my anger. 'The work these people are doing is a complete waste of time', I told him. 'It's not going to protect the bridge from the flood waters. Who on earth organised this work?' It was none other than Mullah Ahmed Zai. When we confronted him he had the audacity to claim that he was merely carrying out my instructions. I wanted to burst into tears, I was so angry and frustrated at the silly, childish way these people behaved. Instead I summoned up my most authoritative air and told the mullah that he was never to work for me on anything again.

After he had left I told Abdul Wahdood exactly what needed to be done to save the bridge. Some more gabions had to be placed either side of the wooden support and then large stones dropped on the downstream side of the support, as the current was likely to undermine the riverbed at that point. Abdul Wahdood asked me if I was paying for this work.

'Certainly not. These people used my wire in a way that I didn't agree to. Now they're going to have to repair the damage they've done.'

'If you do not pay, they will not finish the job.'

I had one last card to play.

'In that case, I won't go back to Gazak. I'm not crossing that bridge while it's in an unsafe condition, and I have to cross it to get up to Gazak. If I don't go to Gazak to inspect the work, there'll be no money for anyone.'

The warlord studied me carefully for a long moment while he assessed how serious I was. He shrugged, 'Tic, tic', which is Urdu for 'OK, OK.' I had won my point. I knew how serious it would be for Abdul Wahdood if the project in Gazak remained unfinished and no one got paid. I also realised that the ultimatum I'd given him could work against me. If the local workers didn't agree to finish the bridge according to my specification, things could go so badly for Abdul Wahdood that he might be deposed. Whoever took over from him might not be so kindly disposed to foreigners and, at best, we could be sent packing immediately; at worst – well, it didn't bear thinking about. The truth of the matter was that we were chronically short of money and I doubted if I could pay for the work on the bridge even if I wanted to.

The next day, tragedy struck. As I walked down to the river I saw, to my horror, that my pride and joy had a yawning gap where the main span had completely disappeared. Just as I had predicted, its wooden support had been washed clean away. I was devastated. I couldn't go to Gazak now and there was very little else that I could usefully do since my reports were all written and my maps drawn. For the next two days Abdul Wahdood kept out of my way. On the third day he came to my house to talk. He pleaded with me to go Gazak; if I didn't, it would jeopardise the whole project. The missing beams would be retrieved from Tsangtmor, the village down river where they had been washed ashore, and no money would be expected for the repairs to the bridge. I didn't want the karez project at Gazak to fail any more than Abdul Wahdood did but the trip up there would be a long one. With our bridge out of action I would have to walk two hours upstream to the village of Danigilzae, where the nearest bridge was located. As there was no alternative, I prepared to leave in the morning.

With Khodai Mir as my bodyguard, I started at seven in the morning. I was still fasting for Ramadan and the journey was even longer than I had anticipated, as flooding forced us to climb high over Bitow mountain. I found Khodai Mir much more helpful than in the past and, with his help, I survived the tortuous paths. By the time we reached Gazak, I was exhausted. A day's march across mountainous terrain on an empty stomach was no joke.

The next few days were the most physically draining of my life. Every day, at three in the morning, I was woken up to partake of peshlomay, which was usually something uneatable at that unearthly hour. Then, at six or seven, I was off on a tour of yet another village and its irrigation systems. Every night was spent in a different house, being kept awake either by the chatter of women and the crying of babies or by the intolerable smoke and heat from some ramshackle wood-burning stove. The trip was agony and I longed to get back to my own little house down in the valley. The only things which kept me going were the huge amount of progress with the work on the karezes and Nur Rajan's constant help and encouragement. Without this I doubt whether I would have kept going. He was always ready to lend me a helping hand up the steep, slippery paths. Most Afghans would never dream of touching a woman other than their wife, and even that not in public. Yet here was this tall, handsome young man showing no inhibitions about taking my arm here and offering his hand there. He seemed very tactile compared to other Afghans and I began to wonder if the rumours I had heard about him were true. We had grown very close, for not only had we been together in Quetta, but it was he who had pulled me from the wrecked lorry all those months ago. It was natural that he should feel protective of me. But here I was, wandering the hills of one of the world's most primitive countries with Mister Tall, Dark and Handsome. I was well aware of the danger inherent in becoming emotionally attached to an Afghan and I thought a great deal about Sarah and Roze Mohammed. I hoped that good common sense would prevail and that no one would get hurt. I certainly had no intention of overstepping the mark.

On this final visit to Gazak an interesting thing happened. While I was up there, a note was delivered to me from Abdul Wahdood passing on a request for me to help the villagers of Tope with their karezes. I had never visited this village as, for a long time, its inhabitants had been bitter enemies of Abdul Wahdood and would have killed anyone venturing onto their land who was associated with him. Nur Rajan, who as usual was my trusty bodyguard, said he would look after me and I was promised safe passage. I remembered being told on my first trip to Gazak that we had to avoid this village because it was a 'bad' place. Now I understood why. I felt nervous although I trusted Nur Rajan's assurance that I would be safe. At Tope I explained to the village elders that I would only pay for work that could be carried out and inspected before I left the valley for good. They readily agreed and Nur Rajan looked relieved, although everyone in the village seemed friendly enough to me.

One morning I stumbled on a scene that reminded me of a typical English village. A group of houses were clustered around a millpond, which was overshadowed by an ancient mulberry tree. Sitting under the tree I soon collected my usual audience of small boys, while the women and girls hovered in the background. All around the village, bedding and carpets were laid out in the sun to air. Nur Rajan told me that the villagers were preparing for Achter, the three-day festival that marked the end of Ramadan. It was only two days to the festival and I was determined to get back to my home in Bitow for it. I pressed on with the work as fast as I could but, after three weeks of not eating properly, I was beginning to feel ill. To add to my troubles, one of the villagers told me that the bridge at Danigilzae, the one we had crossed to get to Gazak, had been washed away. Over and over again I asked him if he was joking. 'No,' came the reply each time. 'The bridge is gone – washed away.' I couldn't believe it. I had no way back. I felt trapped. To crown it all, I woke up the next morning with severe stomach cramps and a feeling that another of my gastric attacks was imminent. I dosed myself with suitable medication, which I never travelled without, and prepared for the arduous journey back to the valley.

Neither Nur Rajan nor myself quite believed that our only route back was cut off. Perhaps they'd got it wrong and the bridge at Danigilzae wasn't really washed away. Maybe they'd got confused with my bridge, which had been destroyed. We started off down the steep paths, and I found myself continually having to lean on Nur Rajan, but he certainly didn't seem to mind. The journey made me extremely hot, as spring was about to give way to summer and this, together with my stomach cramps, kept me in constant discomfort. When we reached the river valley, we stopped at a village there to enquire again about the bridge at Danigilzae. 'No,' we were assured, 'it really has been washed away.' We walked down to the river. When we got there I looked across and could see our house on the other side, several hundred feet away. Nur Rajan suggested that our only course of action was to wade across the river. The idea of a dip in the river to cool down appealed to me so I agreed to try it. Not for a moment did I consider that I might be stepping into extreme danger. But when I looked closely at the crossing, I noticed not only how wide the river was but how brown and filthy it was as well. I still felt uncomfortably hot, so I tied my scarf tightly around my head and waded into the water. It was deliciously cool but I was soon up to my knees and felt the current tugging at me. It was too late to change my mind so, holding Nur Rajan's hand, I started across. The riverbed was covered in small, slippery stones and several times I lost my footing, but my companion kept tight hold of me. As the water got deeper, I wondered if I'd be able to swim with all my clothes on, should the occasion arise. The water reached my neck and I got really frightened.

Nur Rajan's strong arm gripped me around the waist. Although the current was pulling us, he kept surging ahead and somehow we reached the other side. I was elated. I was back home in time for Achter and this was the last day of Ramadan. Thanking my gallant rescuer profusely, I raced to our house as fast as my waterlogged clothes would allow. The last thing I wanted was for the local people to catch sight of me and wonder what I'd been up to. Unfortunately, Abdul Wahdood heard about my little swimming escapade and was very angry. Not for long, though, as he needed my help with his cassette player, which wasn't working. It didn't take me long to discover that all it needed was new batteries. My street cred in the area got another boost and the warlord was my friend once more.

After such a gruelling trip it was wonderful to have a full night's sleep and not to be woken at 3 am. I woke late feeling wonderfully refreshed and free from stomach cramps. It seemed these were not going to develop into something serious after all. I got up eager to join in the Achter festivities, which mark the end of Ramadan, but for me it was an anti-climax. Everyone had visited each other's houses before I was even awake. Sarah told me there had been egg-rolling with coloured hard-boiled eggs, but all I saw were the remnants of the eggshells scattered about the village. The lack of a proper bridge didn't help, and a number of people disapproved of singing and dancing so soon after two funerals.

The Afghans celebrated the end of Ramadan by dressing up in bright new clothes and visiting friends to wish them 'Mubarak', which means 'congratulations'. Roze Mohammed, in a new outfit, was the first to visit us. He called out 'Mubarak achter', before disappearing into the kitchen to talk with Sarah. They certainly seemed to go in for long conversations and, as we didn't like to interrupt, Caroline and I went to the spring to do some washing. We watched people passing by in their new clothes and had fun calling out 'Mubarak achter' to them all. Abdul Wahdood and his family were not in a position to afford new clothes and I felt sorry for this fine young man whose power, like his money, seemed in danger of dwindling away. We heard that fighting had broken out between two rival factions not far from us; Abdul Wahdood would have to go and put a stop to it. His life seemed to lurch from one crisis to another and I hoped that nothing awful would happen to him before our stay in Afghanistan came to an end. We had some good news: a Mujahideen had arrived in the valley from Quetta and would deliver some letters to us the next day. One of these was from Chris. As usual, he addressed us in the most disparaging terms but, more seriously, he told us that there would not be an engineer to replace me as I had hoped. What was I to do? Leave Afghanistan at my appointed time, without seeing my bridge rebuilt or the karezes in Gazak in proper working order? What kind of legacy would I be leaving to show for a year of my life? A few fruit trees and some incomplete irrigation works? I also had letters from my family; they made me feel suddenly homesick. Caroline always had lots of people to talk to because of her work and Sarah had Roze Mohammed. Again I felt very alone.

Chris's letter suggested that I was expected to leave at the same time as Andy, but he said he was happy to travel on his own if I wanted to stay longer. I could leave with Sarah and Caroline at the end of May, by which time the project at Gazak should have been completed to my satisfaction. As for the bridge –sadly, it might not get rebuilt that year. Perhaps if I left adequate instructions the local people would manage the work when the waters were calmer in the autumn.

Before I left I was able to clear up the mystery of the missing five hundred trees. I hadn't seen Abdul Hamid for some time. When he did show up I asked him about the trees. 'I gave them out to the people along the way. It seemed silly not to let them have them as I was passing.' I might have known that there would be a simple explanation and I was pleased that my trust in Abdul Hamid had not been betrayed. He promised to provide me with a list of everyone he'd given a tree to and I looked forward to meeting up with Chris again and setting him straight.

Shortly after this the new team members arrived. Sally was a nurse, Linda was a midwife and Tim was a vet. He had been brought out to teach the local people how to cope with some of the diseases that afflicted their animals. The new team members were accompanied by Rebecca, the monitor sent out by Health Unlimited to check up on us. We had all been dreading her arrival, but she couldn't have appeared less threatening. She was small and softly spoken, but I suspected that beneath that gentle manner lay a very astute brain and an observant eye. She came with me on my final trip to Gazak, where we inspected each item of work to confirm it had been completed satisfactorily. It was wonderful to see each karez cleared and flowing freely. The villagers made a great fuss of us and laid on a magnificent feast. I had earned my nickname of Zurghuna (green lady). First I had brought in the fruit tree saplings, and now I had provided more irrigation water.

I could not rest on my laurels. Back in Bitow Rebecca spent a number of days checking and rechecking my paperwork, especially the accounting side of it. Materials bought and wages paid were put under the magnifying glass. When she had finished I was able to tell Abdul Wahdood that she seemed well satisfied. I reminded him that my work with his enemies in the village of Tope had ended his long-running feud with them and said that, before I left the valley, I wished to ask a favour. I wanted to take Zebedee back to England with me. He refused, saying, 'This will be a very big problem.' Nur Rajan came to my rescue, promising that he would personally take responsibility for my safety and that of the cat. Abdul Wahdood smiled and said, 'Alright, you can take him. You have been a great help to us here in Daichopan. I will grant you this favour in return.'

The last few days in Afghanistan were one mad rush. There were instructions to be given, packing to be done and huge farewell meals to eat. One of these feasts was at the clinic, where I formally presented Abdul Garni with my penknife, which he had attempted to steal. Everyone laughed and clapped, as they knew about the deal I had struck with him all those months ago.

On my last day, I walked down to the river to take photographs of what was left of my bridge. The water was still too high for the repairs to be started and I doubted whether they ever would be. I was surprised how little it worried me. True, I'd come out here to build a bridge and now it was gone. But that was the Afghans' choice. I had told them what to do and they had ignored me. My gabions were still standing firmly on the river bed, proof that my technology worked. There was nothing to feel ashamed of. I walked back to the house with mixed feelings about leaving. At times it had been a real test of endurance and I had felt lonelier than I had imagined possible. There had been times when the locals had so infuriated me that I could cheerfully have throttled every Afghan in the valley. However, I felt more in control of my life than ever before. Out here I had none of the everyday responsibilities I had to face back in England, with constantly ringing telephones and the kind of pressure I wasn't sure I wanted to return to. I would miss the high, wide, open spaces of Gazak and, most of all, I would miss my trusted bodyguard, Nur Rajan. He had been a good friend to me and I knew that he would remember me long after all the others had forgotten.

We collected our belongings together and prepared to get in the jeep. As usual it was going to be a squash. As well as Sarah, Caroline and myself there would be Zebedee. I called out to him but there was no answer. As everyone began a frantic search for the missing cat, I panicked. I felt bereft; he had been my constant companion and comfort in this wild country. Just as I was beginning to give up hope Caroline appeared with him tucked under her arm. She had found him stuck up a tree down by the bridge. As the jeep drove us out of the village on the start of the long, arduous journey into Pakistan, I was so relieved to have Zebedee with me that I had no time to feel sad at leaving. There were three Mujahideen in the front, with Sarah, Caroline, myself and Rebecca, the monitor, squeezed in behind. Zebedee was very unhappy at being shut in a box and scrabbled and howled all the way back to the main Kabul – Kandahar highway. We were forced to let him out and he sat on my lap behaving impeccably for the rest of the journey. As always when travelling through Afghanistan, we were disguised in our head-to-toe burkhas. It wasn't that usual to see a Muslim woman travelling in a jeep, but to see such a person with a cat on her lap was exceptional indeed.

We took the risk and it paid off. The journey proved as hot and dusty as our first drive into Afghanistan months before. As we climbed up into the mountains Abdul Wahdood had described as 'good for hiding in', we passed the site of our horrific accident. I recalled my thoughts at that time, as I lay trapped in the wreckage: 'Why did I ever come on this crazy trip to Afghanistan?' Now I knew. I'd wanted a challenge, and my goodness I had got one! What I didn't realise, as we continued our long and uncomfortable journey to Quetta, was that, when I got there, even greater challenges would be waiting for me.

Chapter Ten

The journey to Quetta was as unbearable as ever. We were sweating and grimy with dust under our suffocating burkhas. With Zebedee fast asleep beneath mine we passed all the Pakistani police checkpoints. I couldn't see Sarah beneath her all-enveloping robes but I was sure she was crying. She had been dreading leaving the valley and Roze Mohammed.

Quetta was dirty and noisy and the air smelt filthy. I had been spoilt by the clean, clear air in our valley, where pollution was non-existent. We arrived at Dr Haqani's guest house around mid-morning and stumbled, tired and dazed, from the car. As soon as we were able, we made for the shower. It took three goes at scrubbing the dirt off before my skin even began to look its normal colour. Sarah and Caroline were very low in spirits while we were in Quetta. Sarah longed to see her family but knew she had to leave Roze Mohammed. Caroline just wanted to get home as quickly as possible, for the news about her father wasn't good. I phoned my parents, who were overjoyed that I was safe and sound and back in relative civilisation. I also called a close friend in England to tell her that I would bring a cat back with me and could she make the arrangements that end for me to import him?

I had several hectic days meeting UN staff and having them check my reports. Chris had spent much of his time in Quetta bad-mouthing the work that we were doing in Daichopan. Now I was able to put my side of the case. I think I convinced them that we had done a good job, but the UNDP staff were more interested in whether I had spent all the money they had given me. Naively I had assumed that the unspent funds could be left in Daichopan so that the project could be continued the following year. Not so. I found myself heavily criticised for not bringing the money back. If only they knew the problems we had faced in such a primitive country. On the few occasions when UN staff did venture into Afghanistan they did so in their luxury Land Cruisers with outriders and full diplomatic status!

It was several days before I discovered the depths to which Chris was willing to sink. Apart from spreading doom and despondency about the project, it appeared that he had been on a spending spree. This came to light as we were going through the project finances. There should have been several thousand pounds in a bank account which Sarah had set up when she had arrived in Pakistan. The account was virtually empty. As soon as Sarah examined the bank records, she discovered the answer. Chris should have paid in money left from his journey from Afghanistan to Quetta. Not only had he not done this, he had more or less emptied the account before disappearing. We later heard he had been sighted in northern Pakistan. This time Chris had done for us. We were broke. We changed our few afghanis into Pakistani currency and worked out whether we had enough to last us until we went home. It would be tight but we thought we'd just manage it.

Despite our poverty, I was determined to keep a promise I had made to Nur Rajan, who had travelled to Quetta with us. I took him to buy a new turban as a thank you for all his help. It was quite an experience. He took me to the bazaar where all the men bought their clothes. There he checked how much I could afford before asking the shopkeeper to bring some for us to look at. Nur Rajan sat on the floor, while the shopkeeper perched on a stool above him and produced paper packets of neatly folded silk taffeta turbans, which he unfurled across the floor with a flourish. Their colours were subdued but beautiful. There were silvers, greys, browns, dark blues and dark greens, all with different sheens and different weaves. I was happy to sit and watch as Nur Rajan tried on one then another, skilfully wrapping them round his head. The shopkeeper held up a mirror, as he turned this way and that, judging their effect. He chose a superb dark blue one, which made him look more like the hero of a romantic novel than ever.

The next day I flew to Islamabad to sort out my visa and was glad to have Rebecca, the monitor, as company. I wasn't sure how I was going to get on. Sarah had an indefinite visa which she had acquired on a previous trip, and Caroline's visitor's visa was still valid, as she had only recently come out from the UK again. They could leave as soon as they were ready and left about a week after we returned to Quetta. I was not in such a fortunate position. My visitor's visa was six months out of date and I couldn't possibly tell the authorities what I had been doing all this time. I thought that as my friend the brigadier had turned out to be head of Military Intelligence, they might know all about my Afghan trip by now; I was terrified of being thrown into a Pakistani jail. I decided to sort out Zebedee's travel papers before my own. This involved much to-ing and fro-ing between the airline office who were to transport him and the Department for Imports and Exports. Fortunately, no one looked too closely at my passport with its out-of-date stamp. After an interminable wait I had Zebedee's export licence and a flight booked and hoped my friend Jenni would arrange everything from the London end. Before braving the visa office, I called at the British Consulate. A charming gentleman there instructed me in the kind of letter I should write to the Department of the Interior. He assured me that it had worked perfectly well for other Health Unlimited staff. All I had to say was that I had not realised that I had to get a visa renewal and I was very sorry and could they please give me an exit visa?

I was not quite so lucky. I presented myself at the Department of the Interior, handed in my passport with the letter and was asked to wait. After ten minutes I was nervous. I was shown in to see a very distinguished-looking person in a very important-looking office. He fired questions at me. 'Why did you allow your visa to overrun? Why didn't you contact this department sooner? Don't you realise that it is illegal for you to remain in this country without a valid visa? What have you been doing in Quetta all this time anyway?' It was a frightening experience.

I decided my best bet was to play a silly, dithering Englishwoman. This wasn't too difficult, as I was already stammering with nerves. I kept playing the part and told him that I'd come to Quetta and fallen in love with the place. I'd liked it so much that I'd just stayed and stayed. That was my story and I stuck to it. Finally, I was told to wait outside while my case was discussed. Eventually the official came out of his office and told me to come back in a week's time. During that period they would investigate my case. This was a disaster. I had my flight booked and now I'd have to postpone it. Suppose they talked to Military Intelligence? How was I going to survive on next to no money? There was nothing I could do about it, so I rearranged both my own flight and Zebedee's. At least it gave me time to get the all-important red sticker from England to go on the cat's cage. This was to show that he had been granted an import licence by the British authorities. Without it, he would be destroyed on arrival in the UK.

I couldn't hang around in Islamabad without money or anywhere to stay, so I returned to Quetta to be greeted with the news that Zebedee had disappeared. At first I wasn't too worried, as I was sure he'd come if I called. I called and called, but he didn't come. I thought that the noise of the traffic and people passing by might be stopping him from hearing me so the next morning I rose early and walked around the streets calling for him. Still no answering 'meow', and I was really worried. The next day Nur Rajan organised some posters in Pashtu for me, offering a reward equivalent to £10, a small fortune for some people in Quetta. As I pinned the posters up on trees and lampposts, people would come up to it, take a look and ask me about the missing cat. They all promised to look out for him, although they must have thought me very strange. In Quetta, cats were not something you kept track of or worried about if you lost them. Several small boys turned up with a variety of cats and were greatly disappointed to learn that none of them was Zebedee. I missed Zebedee so much and would get up at daybreak every morning and look for him before the traffic started. Late at night I'd do the same thing, and repeating the search day after day and night after night began to take its toll on me. I was also worried about my lack of money, as well as the thought of prison looming over me. Much of the time I was close to tears, and wished that Sarah and Caroline were still in Quetta. Nur Rajan was a constant support. When the posters failed to bring a result, he suggested we try advertising on local radio.

When I phoned the radio station I was told that I had to have a police report before they would advertise the lost cat. I wasn't at all keen to report the loss at a police station. The authorities in Islamabad had kept my passport and I wouldn't know what to say if the police asked to see it. However, I couldn't see what other choice I had, so I tracked down the nearest police station and went up to the desk. The tough-looking desk sergeant with a gun at his hip didn't make me feel any easier. 'I want to report a lost cat,' I said. 'Cat?' he queried. 'Yes, you know, cat? meow?' 'You have lost a cat?' I was not getting through to him. 'But there are lots of cats in Quetta,' he continued. 'Yes, I know, but this was a very special cat.' 'Ah, this was pedigree cat? I think a Siamese cat, yes?' 'Well, actually, no. He's just an ordinary ginger cat, but he's very special to me.' The policeman looked at me as if I were mad. He seemed to be trying not to smile. He called a colleague and they went into a huddle. Every now and then I caught the word 'bili', which means 'cat' in Urdu. The desk sergeant crossed back to me and began to take down all Zebedee's particulars: name, colour, age, value. Value? What could I say? Nothing – and yet everything. Eventually I was handed the finished document, a very formal-looking affair. The policeman did it with great solemnity but I sensed that he was struggling not to laugh. Nevertheless, I had my official proof of having reported the missing cat, so I set off by motor rickshaw for the radio station. There I produced my official police document and was escorted to the office of the programme controller, no less. I'm sure that everyone there thought I was just a crazy Englishwoman, but they promised that my loss would be advertised on the radio every hour, four times in English, four times in Urdu and four times in Pashtu.

The following day a further stream of small boys appeared at

Dr Haqani's guest house gate with a selection of cats of all shapes, sizes and colours but, alas, no Zebedee. I went to collect his travelling-box, which I had ordered the week before. The sight of the neatly made wooden container, with its little doors and wire mesh, made me more upset than ever. Time had almost run out and I had less than two days before I had to leave for Islamabad, no matter what. I had already delayed my flight once and it was imperative that I reported back to the Department of the Interior on the appointed day. David and Rachel, a wonderful couple living in the guest house, promised to send Zebedee on to England if they found him, but by now I had given up hope. The next morning David was to give an English lesson to a young boy who helped in the house and he was wondering what they could talk about. I suggested that he could use Zebedee as a topic. 'Jo has lost her cat.' 'Where is her cat?' 'Have you seen her cat?' He thought it was a great idea and tried it out. He was utterly amazed when the boy answered, 'Yes, I have seen Jo's cat.' When we questioned him further he confirmed that he really had seen my cat. On hearing there was a reward, he became very enthusiastic. 'I will bring the cat to you this evening at six o'clock,' he promised. I took this with a pinch of salt and when six o'clock came and there was no knock at the door, I felt my scepticism was justified and resigned myself to never seeing Zebedee again. 'If only I knew what happened to him,' I thought. 'He might be shut in a cellar somewhere, starving to death, or have been killed by a car. I should have left him in Afghanistan.' I started blaming myself for causing his untimely death. At about a quarter past six, there was a banging at the gate and I went to open it. There was the young boy, holding a startled Zebedee. I couldn't believe my eyes. I took him and hugged him to me. He was safe and sound at last. The boy said that the cat had been shut in a nearby empty house that he acted as caretaker for. Having paid over the promised reward, I shut Zebedee in the house and swore he would never leave it again, except in his travelling-box.

The next day, Nur Rajan went with me to the airport with Zebedee safely shut up in his travelling-box. He stopped outside the terminal building. I climbed out with the cat-box and my luggage, expecting him to come into the building to see me off. But he elected to say goodbye, right there and, as he did so, grasped my hand in his and held it for a long time. I thought it strange for, although we had become such close friends, we had never touched in this way. The moment seemed to go on and on but then, knowing I could delay no longer, I forced myself to break free, smiled at him and walked into the terminal. I would probably never see Nur Rajan again.

As soon as I arrived in Islamabad, I went to the Ministry of the Interior, praying that they would give me an exit visa. As I waited nervously outside the official's office, I thought to myself, "After all I've been through these past twelve months, ending up in a foreign jail would be the last straw." I was in luck though. Whether the man I was dealing with was in a good mood that day, or whether my carefully worded letter of apology had done the trick, I shall never know. Whatever it was, I was let off with a stern warning and had my passport returned to me, together with a letter for me to take to the Immigration Office, instructing them to stamp my exit visa.

There was one last hurdle to clear – the red sticker for Zebedee's travel- box, the one to show he had a British import licence. The sticker had to be couriered from England and I thought I had successfully organised this, except that I had to leave Quetta before it arrived there. At the courier's office in Islamabad, I explained how important the package was. Like everyone else in that part of the world, they couldn't understand how a mere cat could be of any importance whatsoever. I was desperate. His life depended on my getting that red sticker on his box. After much pleading on the phone with the head office of the courier firm, they finally managed to track it down and get it redirected to Islamabad, where it arrived on the morning of Zebedee's departure. That cat seemed destined always to leave things until the last minute.

My last few days in Islamabad were miserable. I didn't know a soul there and I had almost no money left. I thought I had calculated exactly how much money I would need between leaving Afghanistan and arriving back in England. However, I hadn't reckoned on the extra days hanging around in Pakistan and all the additional expenses incurred with Zebedee. I was worried about excess baggage charges and so had to keep some money for that. I worked out the cost of the hotel and transport to the airport and realised that I wouldn't have anything left to buy food during my two days in Islamabad. In desperation, I phoned England and asked the Health Unlimited office for help. They arranged for another charity in Islamabad to loan me some money and I went straight round to collect it. The official there was very kind and, when he heard I was all on my own in the city, he invited me to dinner that evening.

I was so thankful for the invitation for, having seen Zebedee onto the plane that day, the last thing I wanted was to be alone. The cat had behaved impeccably, although he hated being in the box. The first thing I'd had to do was take him in to the Lufthansa office; this proved much harder than I had expected. The airline's office was in an arcade of shops inside a luxury hotel. At the main door I was stopped by a liveried doorman, who informed me that I wasn't allowed to take a pet into the hotel. He refused to listen to my explanation and I had to leave Zebedee at the entrance to the hotel while I fetched an official from the Lufthansa office to vouch for me and the cat. He escorted both of us to the Lufthansa office, where Zebedee was duly weighed. I went, complete with the airline's waybill and the cat, to the customs. They filled in reams of paperwork and, with the help of a little financial inducement, allowed me to take Zebedee back to the hotel for a few hours instead of leaving him in the hot freight department at the airport. When it was time to take him back to the airport for his departure, the official let me take him out to the luggage cart myself. There I gently placed him on top of all the other baggage and stayed until the cart was driven off. As he looked back at me with a plaintive 'meow', I just hoped he would have a good flight.

I followed Zebedee the next day and was met at Heathrow airport in London by my friend Jenni. I stayed with her for the next few days, as I felt disorientated. I found the traffic and the shops overwhelming. I had to walk out of Sainsbury's food store because the huge choice was too much for me. When I had returned to Quetta from Daichopan, the small shops on the high street there had seemed like emporiums. I realised how cut off I had been all that time.

Because I had stayed longer in the valley than originally intended, I had to start work only days after setting foot back in Britain. I would so have loved a holiday, not having had a break of any sort since well before going to Afghanistan. Although I was feeling traumatised, I had to complete my final report, visit my parents, buy some new clothes for work and move back into my house in Oxford, all before starting back at work. When I visited my parents the day after arriving back in England, I realised for the first time just how worried they had been while I was away. It must have been terribly difficult for them, getting such infrequent mail from me. That night they took me out to a restaurant where I ate pork for the first time in a year.

Soon after I got back to England, I managed to phone Nur Rajan in Quetta. It was a strange sensation, talking to him from London and wondering what he would have made of it, if he'd been there with me. He said he'd had a letter from Daichopan and that everyone was fine and he'd be going back there shortly. After I'd hung up I felt as if I'd been watching a good film. While it was showing I'd really enjoyed it and been completely involved in it but, when the film finished, that was it – everything was over and I was back in the real world. It was difficult to realise that everything was still there, exactly as I had left it: my bridge waiting to be rebuilt, the new karezes in Gazak carrying water to the crops and my trees sprouting and growing.

I spent much of my first week back at the Health Unlimited offices, writing a final report and having a debriefing with Roger Doran. I was very angry when I arrived there, for I discovered a pile of things in the office that people had sent there to be forwarded to me. These were little things, costing next to nothing to post, but which would have added so much to my comfort: batteries for my camera, new earphones and packets of boiled sweets. The sweets would have made great presents for the Afghans. No one seemed to care that I had been left on my own in

Islamabad with hardly any money, not knowing if I would finish up in jail. They also seemed unappreciative of what I had achieved out there and the huge difficulties I had overcome. Back at Thames Water, the staff were just as indifferent to where I'd been and what I'd achieved. While I'd been away the interior of the building had been completely reorganized. On my first day back, I stood in the main foyer trying to guess where I was supposed to go. Someone I had previously worked with walked by. As he passed me he smiled and called out, 'Hi Jo. Where are you working these days?' He hadn't realised that I'd been away! So much for working in a big organisation. I found it extremely difficult to explain, even to people I knew well, what I had been through and how I had changed because of it.

When I returned to my own house, walking around inside gave me a strange feeling. I suppose I was admitting to myself that the adventure was over. Certainly I was pleased to be back in my old home, but there was a sadness in me and I found it hard to settle.

Now that I was back at work, there remained the problem of what job I was going to do. Before I left for Afghanistan I had helped to set up a plumbing company for Thames Water. Now I found myself in the post of Sales and Marketing Manager there. If I'd tried, I couldn't have found a job more different from the one I'd been doing for the past year in Afghanistan. Just going shopping was a culture shock for me. Selling plumbing services seemed a ridiculous use of my time and my heart wasn't in it. I knew what I wanted – a practical job using my engineering training and experience. I wanted a job in operations. That had been one of my main reasons for wanting to get experience abroad.

I went to see the Personnel Manager and asked about jobs in Operations. He said a manager was required for one of the company's largest sewage works, located in South London. My heart leapt, but then I realised he was joking. He thought I was too. He couldn't believe that I wanted a works-based job. Tentatively he mentioned that there was a vacant job based at Farmoor, near Oxford, but it was a grade below the one I was currently on. I wasn't sure what to do. Twice in the past I had applied unsuccessfully for jobs at this very works and had been told, unofficially, that being female counted against me. Twice before I had consciously decided against applying for lower-graded jobs there, even though it would have been a way into operations. I didn't see why I should, when my male counterparts did not have to. If I went back to Oxford, would I slip into the comfy, cosy rut that I'd managed to break out of? On the other hand, I knew I'd love the job; it was what I'd always wanted to do.

I was in two minds when I went to be interviewed for the job – and it was a disaster. My prospective boss, the Divisional Manager, told me I had to expect to take a downgrading as I had no experience of managing manual labour. I was incensed; what were Afghan well-diggers if not manual labour? Were British manual workers really so strange that managing them was a bigger cultural shock than managing Mullah Ahmed Zai? My interviewer didn't seem the slightest bit interested in the work I'd been doing over the last ten months. In fact, he seemed to regard it as some little jaunt I'd been on, something to be treated as a minor aberration.

That was it! All the trauma of my last few weeks in Pakistan, the lack of a holiday, the lack of any appreciation on my return, my difficulties at adjusting to civilisation again, came forcefully to a head. I lost my temper. It was not characteristic of me at all but I can see full well why I did. How I got the job after that I'll never know, but somehow I persuaded the Divisional Manager to give me a trial period in the post. Within a month of arriving back in England I was where I'd wanted to be ever since I entered the water industry – managing a plant. The self-confidence I'd gained from rising to new challenges and overcoming countless difficulties stood me in good stead in my job as the first ever female water treatment works manager.

Gradually I settled back into civilised life. It helped to be able to visit Zebedee while he was in quarantine, although I wasn't allowed to see him for the first fortnight, until he settled into his new surroundings. I hardly recognised him. His coat was glossy and the fur had grown again on his tail where he had burnt it on the stove. As soon as I sat down, he climbed up on my lap and began to wash himself contentedly.

I'll never forget my time in Afghanistan and I shall never forget Afghanistan. Sometimes I miss Daichopan so much it hurts but, with the passage of time many of my memories have faded somewhat, rather like my ability to speak Pashtu.

When I'd been back for almost a year, I was woken very early by a telephone call. 'This is Pakistan. I have a person-to-person call for Jo Parker.'

It was Sarah; she was back working in Quetta. Perhaps she wanted to get as near to Afghanistan as she could. Perhaps she had some wild idea of meeting up with Roze Mohammed again. It was wonderful to be able to exchange news and she was thrilled that I was doing the job I'd always wanted to do, even if it was down a grade. Then she said, 'I've got someone here who wants to speak to you,' and on the line came Nur Rajan, Mister Tall, Dark and Handsome. He was on a training course in Quetta and Sarah had organised the telephone call. I found myself stumbling over my words, partly because it was so early in the morning, partly because I'd forgotten so much of my Pashtu and partly because I was so taken aback to hear his voice. He had done so much to help me and I felt I had done so little. He asked hesitantly if I was married and I remembered that I had, for my own protection, told the Afghans when I first met them that I was engaged to be married. To keep up the pretence, I found myself answering 'yes' to his question. There was a long pause and I could tell that he was crestfallen. How crazy it was. He was a man from a far-off, primitive land and I was an English lady managing a water plant. We said goodbye and that was the last I ever heard of him.

Shortly after the telephone conversation with Nur Rajan I received a letter from Abdul Wahdood.

Dear Jo

How are you? We are all fine in Afghanistan. The fighting with the Hazarah is now finished and we have all had a good rest. I hope that Zebedee is also happy. I hear that you have put Zebedee in a special prison. Your friend Mullah Ahmed Zai is also fine, he is now washing a little. He all the time says 'Where is Jo? Where is my salary?' Thank you for your work in Daichopan and we hope you come back. This year we have had 12,000 trees and none have been lost and we are still giving to people. Greetings to your family and your friends.

Abdul Wahdood

He never wrote again, although I heard from one of the aid agencies that he, and his Mujahideen, had become supporters of the Taliban. As the Taliban took hold, most aid workers were withdrawn. At last things there are improving so, as the Afghans would say, 'Ze zuruck barazum, Inshallah.' I will go back, God willing.